AF346171

DevOps Flow: Code to Production

Naina

Copyright © 2024 by Naina

All rights reserved. No part of this book may be reproduced in any manner whatso-ever without written permission except in the case of brief quotations embodied in critical articles and reviews.

First Printing, 2024

Table of Contents

Chapter 1: Introduction

1.1 Background and Problem Statement

It is has become a normal trend that many software development organizations organize their work in team-based structures (Kirsch, Ko, & Haney, 2010). The motives being that the nature of work is becoming increasingly complex, knowledge-intensive and inconstant (Wiedemann & Wiesche, 2018). With teams working well together, organizations can react quickly to the rapidly changing environment. According to Wiesche and Kremar (2014), these teams require individuals with a balanced set of knowledge and skills. However, it is an objective that is difficult to achieve, to get these teams to work together effectively and efficiently in support of organizational goals.

One possibility to achieve this objective is through better team synergy between development and operations teams. According to Zoltan (2012) and Hackman (1983), team synergy describes a collective and supportive action within the team that generates additional drive beyond what can be achieved by an individual. Studies have shown that team synergy determines how team members interact to augment significant team outcomes, such as innovation (Zhang, 2016; Paulus & Kenworthy, 2017), team engagement, and involvement (Smith, Wallace, Vandenberg, & Mondore, 2018). Furthermore, the study of Zoltan (2012) and that of Tymon and Stumpf (2003) reveals that team social capital is the basis for the creation of team synergy. Therefore, building social capital is critical to the success of the team, it must occur before team synergy can be established.

Not long ago the use of Agile methods in software projects gained so much popularity, that it has become the principal driver for performance within many IT operations (Cram & Newell, 2016). However, software development projects continue to be a major concern for software development teams (Macnab & Doctolero, 2019). Today, many organizations are adopting an approach called DevOps that goes beyond agile (Rose et al., 2016). DevOps combines development and IT operations and extends the agile principles beyond the boundaries of developing code to the entire delivered service (Mullaguru,2015). Because of DevOps, organizations can shorten their software release cycles to hours and deliver new software features within a short period of time (Sebastian et al., 2017). DevOps is increasingly becoming a *de facto* standard in the industry. Every year, more and more software companies report improvements on their development process and ability to deliver value-added services (Bruel & Jiménez, 2018).

Many organizations are adopting this approach to benefit from cost reduction, high innovation throughput, fast time to market and quality improvements (Kim, 2014). One of the challenges facing DevOps adopters is the clash of priorities between development and IT operations personnel (Nybom, Smeds, & Porres, 2016). IT operations require more stability and security and suggest that developers should not change software products frequently, while developers are more concerned with delivering new software features to customers quickly (Yiran & Yilei,

2017). Within DevOps teams, barriers between development and IT operations personnel could appear due to challenges associated with project governance, people, processes, and technology (Jonker, 2017). There is a need to solve these problems to achieve team synergy (Fitzgerald & Stol, 2017). According to Liu, Wang, and Chua (2015), complex assignments need to be dealt with by the team and calls for effective collaboration, shared values, social cohesion and understanding among team members.

1.2 Research Questions and Objectives

The research questions for this study are as follows:

Main research question:

> What are the factors that influence the synergy between software development and IT operations in a DevOps environment?

Sub questions:

1. What factors are enablers of relational, structural and cognitive dimensions of social capital as a basis for team synergy between development and IT operations?

2. What factors are inhibitors of relational, structural and cognitive dimensions of social capital as a basis for team synergy between development and IT operations?

The objectives of this study are as follows:

1. To identify the factors that influence the synergy between development and IT operations within a DevOps environment.

2. To identify which one of the factors identified promote the synergy between development and IT operations.

3. To identify which one of the factors identified inhibit the synergy between development and IT operations.

1.3 Significance of Study

The information gathered in this study will contribute to research and the industry by helping to distinguish the factors that influence the synergy between development and operations teams in a DevOps environment. The factors identified in this study will give insights into how organizations can influence the build and motivate their DevOps teams in order to achieve team synergy. This research will also help indicate what factors are significant in promoting the three dimensions of team social capital and those that inhibit the dimensions of team social capital.

The study will strengthen the need for team synergy in DevOps teams and provide an understanding of the role of team social capital in building team synergy.

1.4 Research Method

This study follows a constructivist approach. In the constructivist approach, the researcher and the participants interact during data collection and therefore knowledge is constructed through the lens of the researcher's interpretation of data (Markey, Tilki, & Taylor, 2014). The study is exploratory since the research attempted to explore the factors that influence the synergy between development and operations teams within a DevOps environment in the form of a case study. The research strategy was a qualitative case study, exploratory in nature. The data collection and analysis were guided by a theoretical framework for team social capital as basis for organisational team synergy (Zoltan, 2012). The research strategy used semi-structured interviews of DevOps team members from a leading information and communication technology service provider in South Africa. The interviews were recorded and uploaded into Nvivo software for transcription and coding. A thematic analysis technique was used for analysing the data collected to extract themes and finally report on the factors that emerged from the data.

1.5 book Overview

This chapter introduced the study for the book as a whole, presented an overview of the background and problem statement, outlined the purpose of the study, stated the research question and study significance, and defined conceptual definitions used during the course of this book research. Chapter 2 reviews the literature, from which a theoretical model is derived, as well as research questions and objectives. Chapter 3 defines the research methodology, paying attention to important issues such as reliability and validity of the study. Chapter 4 presents the empirical findings for this study. Chapter 5 discusses the findings in the context of research questions, literature and their implications to theory and literature. Finally, Chapter 6 concludes the study and recommends directions for future research.

Chapter 2: Literature Review

This chapter presents the literature review within which this study is positioned. The literature highlights areas that have been addressed regarding the factors that influence team synergy between development and IT Operations teams. The literature review is divided into several sections. Section 2.1 presents literature on team synergy; Section 2.2 presents literature on team social capital. Section 2.3 presents literature on the DevOps concept followed by section 2.4 which discusses the theoretical framework to be used throughout the study.

2.1. Team Synergy

Team synergy is a combined collaborative effort within a team that creates additional energy beyond what an individual could accomplish (Zoltan, 2012). Hackman (1983) substantiates that synergy emerges from interacting team members and influences the ability of the team to deal with the challenges and prospects in its performance objectives. His normative model of team effectiveness suggests that team synergy facilitates team effectiveness through its support for team interaction by applying ways that reduce process losses and maximize process gains (Salas, Dickinson, Converse & Tannenbaum, 1992). Process losses emerge from insufficient coordination and lack of motivation, and process gains develop through a shared commitment to the team and its work (Hackman, 1983). Process losses, for instance, cognitive biases like groupthink, negatively affect team decision making in software development teams (Coyle, Conboy, & Acton, 2013; Brown, 2014). On the other hand, Deek and McHugh (2007) described process gains as factors that increase performance in a collaborative environment, which include synergies and learning that occur in a team environment. In the context of software development, process gains occur when team members feel valued, respected, and involved in decision-making (Kahn, 2014). To foster team synergy, the involvement of various development stakeholders such as developers, operations personnel, testers, designers, and database experts in the software development process is very critical (Alnaji & Salameh, 2015).

The existence of synergy in a team stimulates and inspires team members and in turn paves way for diversity and openness to ideas (Zoltan, 2012). Previous studies agree that new possibilities and innovative ways of doing work are discovered through synergy (Covey, 1990; Hoegl, & Gemuenden, 2001). Innovation brings about success in software development teams, which contributes to team efficiency and the personal satisfaction of team members (Rose, Jones, & Furneaux, 2016). The association between team synergy with modern software development practices, such as Agile and DevOps, is seen through team cooperation, collaboration, team support (Hemon, Lyonnet, Rowe, & Fitzgerald, 2019) and mutual learning (Wiedemann, & Schulz, 2017). While prior research noted that synergetic relationships bring about team effectiveness and productivity (Lick, 2006), Zoltan (2012) argued that most teams fail to achieve team synergy due to circumstances emerging from shortcomings in the dimensions of team social capital, such as group thinking.

2.2. Team Social Capital

Putnam (1995) describes the concept of social capital as social ties, norms and trust, which facilitates team members to participate or act together to pursue shared objectives effectively. Team social capital brings up the quality of interaction between people in a team and improves the way they perform team activities and collectively comply with norms while depending on the social environment as a source of rights and obligations (Zoltan, 2012). Through team social capital, team members can derive a sense of mutual obligation, social trust, shared norms, shared language, mutual support, and network ties of goodwill (Huysman, & Wulf, 2004; Meng, Clausen, & Borg, 2018). The studies observed social capital as a collective resource that manifests itself in organizations where it affects opportunities for team collaboration and social support, which eventually forms team synergy.

Social capital produces synergy for creative cooperation among team members (Sozbilir, 2018), which implies that there is a strong bond between team social capital and team synergy. Zoltan found it unlikely to talk about team synergy and even less about the results of the team without the elements representing the dimensions of team social capital, which researchers classified as structural, relational and cognitive dimensions (Lee, Park, & Lee, 2013). The study of Davis and Daniels (2016) and that of Wiedemann and Schulz (2017) recognizes the value and influence of team social capital on software development teams, especially DevOps teams. Team social capital influences team performance in software development teams by increasing the team's ability to integrate knowledge (Robert Jr, Dennis, & Ahuja, 2008), solving complex problems (Smite, Moe, Sablis, & Wohlin, 2017), facilitating coordination, collaboration, and resource exchange (Alsharo, Gregg, & Ramirez, 2017).

2.2.1. Structural Dimension

The structural dimension describes the types of relationships between the team members based on the existence of social patterns and structures created for one purpose, which may serve another purpose (Nahapiet & Ghoshal, 1998). These social structures and patterns are channels used to exchange information and share resources. Tsai and Ghoshal (1998) defined the structural dimension based on social interaction between people in an organization outside their work environment, which is their history of social ties. Several studies associated with team collaboration have observed that people's previous social ties can predict present or future collaborations (Defazio, Lockett, & Wright, 2009; Pinheiro, Pinho, & Lucas, 2015). The reason being, there is an enhanced perception of the value of collaboration. Strong social ties as observed in DevOps practices facilitate team synergy by bringing activities of software development and operation closer together and encourage continuous team collaboration. (Sacks, 2012; Hoda, Salleh, & Grundy, 2018; Wiedemann & Wiesche, 2018).

In literature, there is no agreed classification regarding the elements of the structural dimension of team social capital. Zoltan (2012) identified team cohesion and coordination to be the primary components forming the structural dimension of social capital while, Lee et al. (2013, 2015) observed social ties, network structure, and organization as elements that form the structural dimension of team social capital. Social ties describe the extent to which team members are connected to their social relationships, the stronger their social ties are, the more interactions between the team members can be made. All the same, team cohesion reflects the synergistic interactions (social ties) between these team members, which involve positive communication, conflict resolution, and effective distribution of work.

2.2.2. Relational Dimension

The relational dimension embraces inter-team relationships that formed through mechanisms of trust, collaboration, engagement, relational norms, and mutual identification (Lee et al., 2013; Zoltan, 2012; Nahapiet & Ghoshal, 1998). When teams have the same view on how to collaborate, a shared understanding is likely to happen. Lang, Dickinson, and Buchal (2002) focused on identifying cognitive factors that affects team collaboration and its effectiveness. Some of the factors found were shared memories, cognitive synchronization, shared meaning, communication, knowledge information, methodologies and management of tasks. Studies have shown that collaboration is positively influenced by trust (Frasquet, Calderón, & Cervera, 2012) and that trust significantly contributes to the functioning of the team through communication and enthusiasm (Joshi, Lazarova, & Liao, 2009). A high level of trust (Ghilic-Micu & Stoica, 2003) and engagement (Zoltan, 2012) are elements of the relational dimension of social capital, founding team synergy. Research focused on engagement suggests that psychological (meaningfulness, availability and safety) conditions (Kahn, 1990) of personal engagement affects the way people inhabit their roles while Macey and Schneider (2008) still argues about unclearness in the definition of engagement in literature. Thus far, Harter, Schmidt and Hayes (2002) described engagement as team or personal involvement, satisfaction and enthusiasm for work. When people feel worthwhile, valuable, and that their contribution is meaningful, they become more engaged.

2.2.3. Cognitive Dimension

The cognitive dimension relates to shared interpretations (e.g. shared language and stories) and systems of meaning (e.g. culture) among organisations or team members who created a relationship (Lee, Park, & Lee 2013; Nahapiet & Ghoshal, 1998). For example, adopted words or terminology frequently used between development and operations teams. The crucial components forming this dimension have been identified in literature as knowledge sharing, transactive memory and shared mental models (Zoltan, 2012). Knowledge is derived from people when they reason or work with information (Bakker, Leenders, Gabbay, Kratzer, & Van Engelen, 2006). Knowledge sharing is a team process, achieved when team members share task relevant ideas, suggestions and information among themselves (Srivastava, Bartol, & Locke, 2006). This process helps categorize an organization's available knowledge repositories and serves as abstracts for transactive memory. Wegner (1985) describes transactive memory as a system where teams collectively encode, store and retrieve knowledge. Shared knowledge facilitates the creation of shared mental models subsequently enables benefits on team coordination and achieves a higher team performance (Smith-Jentsch, Mathieu, & Kraiger, 2005).

2.3 The Concept of DevOps

This section discusses the concept of DevOps in terms of the perceived definitions (2.3.1), the values (2.3.2) DevOps brings the industry and research, the most relevant approaches (2.3.3) of DevOps, the challenges (2.3.4) faced in DevOps environment that are linked to the research area and finally the factors that influence team synergy derived from section 2.2 ,where social capital and its dimensions were discussed.

2.3.1 Definition of DevOps

The term first appeared in 2009 while Patrick Debois was setting up a DevOpsDays conference in Belgium (Hutterman, 2012). However, there is contradicting evidence as to when DevOps first emerged. Some researchers claim that DevOps has been established since 2007 (Erich, Amrit, & Daneva, 2014). While DevOps gained so much publicity in the software industry, the concept still lacks an agreed definition. There are varying viewpoints in the literature regarding what DevOps is (Dyck, Penners, & Lichter, 2015). Some researchers define DevOps as a cultural movement that consists of multiple practices aiming at developing more flexibility and effectiveness within business processes (Walls, 2013; Erich et al., 2017). Jabbari, bin Ali, Petersen, and Tanveer (2016) explored the definitions for DevOps in literature and identified fundamental components that define DevOps (see Table 2.3).

Table 2.3: Components of DevOps definition (adapted from Jabbari et al., 2016)

	Component	Definition of Component
C1	Development and Operations	The term DevOps has been coined by a combination of Development and Operations (or Developers and Operators
C2	Communication, Collaboration and Team Working	DevOps is defined as a paradigm or method or set of principles and/or practices that enables communication and collaboration resulting in efficient team working between developers and operators
C3	Bridge the gap	DevOps is defined as a paradigm or method or set of principles and/or practices that bridges the gap (as the main goal of DevOps) between development and operations. This component is in a close correlation with C2 in the literature
C4	Development method	DevOps is defined as a modern software development method to respond to the inter-dependencies between development and operations by unifying modern methods and tools resulting in a real convergence between developers and operators
C5	Software Delivery	DevOps is defined as a paradigm or set of principles focuses on software delivery through enabling continuous feedback, quick response to changes and using automated delivery pipelines resulting in reduced cycle time. De Bayser, Azevedo and Cerqueira (2015) have explicitly mentioned that DevOps was born for fast delivery of web-based systems
C6	Automated deployment	DevOps is defined as a paradigm or set of principles that enables automating deployment process from the source code in version control to the production environment
C7	Continuous integration	Devops is defined as a practice that emphasizes the tasks enabling continuous integration between software development and its operational deployment needs
C8	Quality assurance	DevOps is defined as a method that combines the concerns of quality assurance with operations and development practices to improve performance

2.3.2. DevOps Principles

Kim, Behr and Spafford (2014) described the principles of DevOps in three categories namely, systems thinking, feedback loops and a culture of continuous experimentation and learning. On the other hand, Humble & Molesky (2010) suggested Culture, Automation, Measurement and Sharing (CAMS) framework as the basis to understand the fundamental concepts behind DevOps. In later research, the CAMS framework was later extended to include services, quality and standards (Erich et al., 2014).   All the same, Lwakatare et al. (2015) also mention four different principles of DevOps, almost similar to the CAMS framework, consisting of Culture, Automation, Measurement and Monitoring. From these studies, it is clear that DevOps has varying principles and different methodologies can be applied with it. DevOps is regarded as an extended version of Agile, therefore Agile principles are applicable. It is important for this research to understand the core principles of DevOps to identify how each of the CAMS affects the synergy between development and operations and the challenges the teams experience when addressing each principle.

2.3.3 DevOps Practices

DevOps practices materialize those principles into daily development and operations activities (de França, Jeronimo Junior, & Travassos, 2016). Therefore, observing the running practices enables the organization to recognize the maturity of DevOps. De França et al. (2016) observed several recommended practices in the context of DevOps. They identified commonalities and grouped them into three main classes: common, development, and operations. Common practices refer to collaborative (Limoncelli & Hughe, 2011; Humble, 2012; Forsgren Velasquez, Kim, Kersten, & Humble, 2014), services and procedural (Duvall, 2012; Erich et al., 2014; Mohamed, 2015) practices which are performed by both development and operations teams. Development practices include continuous integration and deployment (Forsgren et al., 2014; Waller, Ehmke, & Hasselbring, 2015), in which the development team consistently merge their code multiple times per day into a central code repository. Finally, operations consist of practices that are performed by the system administrators such as infrastructure configuration management and automation. Although, some researchers argue that DevOps has no clear consensus regarding the set of recommended practices (de França et al., 2016; Stahl, Martensson, & Bosch, 2017), most of the identified practices are performed by development and operations teams together.

2.3.4 DevOps Adoption Challenges

The main aim is to combine development and operations, with a fundamental goal of shortening the feedback loop and the development cycle through synergy, automation, and frequent software releases (Humble & Farley, 2010; Lwakatare et al.,2016). However, due to many challenges encountered in the adoption of DevOps, these objectives are not always met. Previous studies have indicated that some of these challenges relate to resistance to change (Prodan, Prodan, & Purcarea, 2015), communication (Lwakatare et al., 2015), cultural matters, ambiguity in the definition of DevOps (Jabbari et al.,2016), complex technical infrastructure, and organizational (Bucena & Kirikova, 2017).

Resistance may occur in many ways, introducing difficulties related to people, processes and technological changes (Prodan et al., 2015). Usually, resistance to change is expected to occur when people are introduced to new ways of working. The operations team that may resist changes because of a lack of awareness of what the development team is doing (Jones, Noppen, & Lettice, 2016). Another common obstacle is that some people seem comfortable with old processes, and they do not realize the need to change (Huttermann, 2012). DevOps depends on a variety of tools to build software delivery pipelines. However, the integration of these tools can prove problematic and challenging to integrate and maintain due to resistance to change (Gill, Loumish, Riyat, & Han, 2018).

Communication challenges between development and operations personnel presents limitations for knowledge sharing between the teams (Lwakatare et al., 2015). It becomes difficult for the DevOps teams to have shared obligations towards the final product as team members prefer their previous responsibilities, which were silo driven (Gill et al., 2018). Diel, Marczak and Cruzes (2016) also pointed out that the Dev vs. Ops mentality will give rise to communication challenges between the development and operations teams, which negatively affect their collaboration and the feedback loop.

The ambiguity in the definition of DevOps also makes the adoption of DevOps challenging. According to Riungu-Kalliosaari et al. (2016), the current lack of consensus concerning the real meaning of DevOps makes the adoption difficult because practitioners might not know which practices they implement for DevOps. Similarly, Stahl, Martensson, and Bosch (2017) explained that for a practitioner, as long as any attempt to investigate how DevOps might benefit one's software development efforts begins by deciding what DevOps is, learning by example and making informed decisions becomes very challenging indeed.

The adoption of DevOps also highlights cultural matters, which creates problems with adapting organizational processes to DevOps (Bucena & Kirikova, 2017). Riungu-Kalliosaari et al. (2016) noted that profound changes to the cultural mindset are required, and the longstanding organizational culture can be a challenge. Merging roles and responsibilities shift means that people have to rethink their established roles (Nybom et al., 2016). The development team has to tackle duties they are not familiar with and might have limitations on accepting new responsibilities. At the same time, operations people may not trust the development team take-over their work or overloaded with handling more frequent releases. Making people change their behavior and beliefs can be difficult, especially if they have had long careers (Walls, 2013; Riungu-Kalliosaari et al., 2016).

The complex technical infrastructure, in particular environments such as databases used in production systems, can be complex enough to make replicating the environments for verification and testing difficult (Riungu-Kalliosaari et al.,2016; Bucena & Kirikova, 2017). As a result, automated testing becomes less reliable, which imply that complex environments provide a challenge for successful DevOps adoption.

2.4 Theoretical Framework

The theoretical framework, presented in Figure 2.4, has been adopted to show the connection between team social capital dimensions and team synergy. The factors influencing team synergy are the constructs feeding into the dimensions of social capital, which form team synergy.

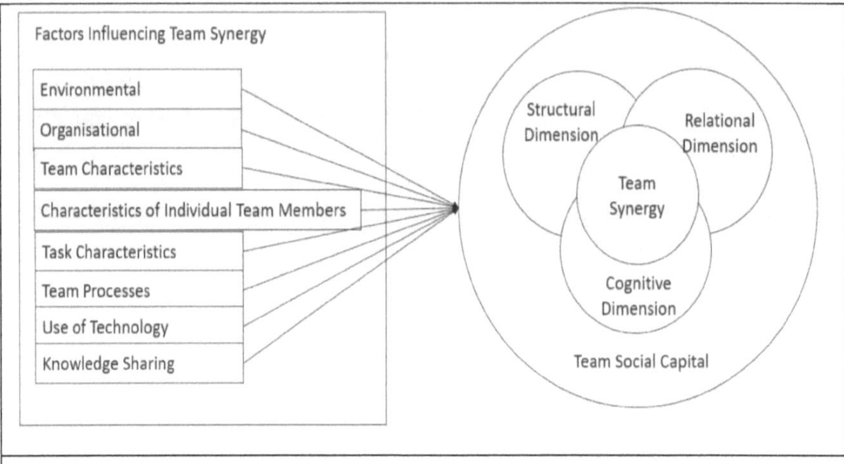

Figure 2.4: Theoretical Framework for Team Synergy in DevOps

2.4.1 Factors Influencing Team Synergy

The literature reviewed that some of the key factors that improve or prevent team synergy are environmental, organizational, characteristics of the team, individual team members, the task characteristics, team processes and knowledge sharing. The previous sections of the literature review were instrumental in deriving these factors through examining the current knowledge on team synergy, team social capital, the concept of DevOps, and the current challenges facing IT practitioners when adopting DevOps. The following sections will give more insight into how these factors are significant to the theoretical framework.

2.4.1.1 Environmental

Research highlights that environmental factors are situational or contextual and they affect individual team members' decision-making behavior in software projects (Jia, Zhang, & Capretz, 2016). An environment consists of the physical space that individuals and teams operate in, the socio-cultural aspects of the workplace and the work organization (Patel, Pettitt, & Wilson, 2012). Extreme environments, for example, prohibit the occurrence of team synergy. Driskell, Salas, and Driskell (2018) described extreme environment settings as significant tasks, social, or environmental demands that entail a high level of risk and increased consequences for poor team performance. Differences between the working environments introduce challenges that affect the synergy between development and operations (Amaradri & Nutalapati, 2016). Software developers are more familiar with the development environment whereas operations personnel are used to the production environment. These environments have a completely different setup. Development environments do not reflect the same configurations as production environments (Bucena & Kirikova, 2017).

2.4.1.2 Organizational

March and Simon (cited in Tsoukas and Knudsen, 2003: 613) defined an organization as a "system of co-ordinated action among individuals and groups whose preferences, information, interests or knowledge differ". An organization is composed of a set of roles and responsibilities that represent it as well as the interaction protocols that occurs between the roles (Zambonelli, Jennings, & Wooldridge, 2000). The foundation, structure, and the functional boundaries of the team are defined by the roles (Patel, Pettitt, & Wilson, 2012). Organizational factors are indispensable ingredients in the success of DevOps teams. Challenges such as lack of constant support and structural change of the organization prevent the synergy between the development and operations teams through limited collaboration (Wang & Liu, 2018).

2.4.1.3 Team Characteristics

De Jong, Dirks and Gillespie (2016) categorized team characteristics as task interdependence, team virtuality, temporal stability, authority differentiation, and skill differentiation. Team virtuality is the degree to which team members work in geographically dispersed locations and different time zones (De Guinea, Webster, & Staples, 2012). Unlike collocated teams, there are no face-to-face communication and close collaboration between the team members in distributed teams. Communication and collaboration are essential elements to the dimensions of team social capital and team synergy (Frasquet et al., 2012). Team Temporal stability is the degree to which team members have a history of working together in the past and an expectation of working together in the future (Lee, Koopman, Hollenbeck, Wang, & Lanaj, 2015). It is linked to the lifespan of the team. Wildman et al. (2012) noted that a shorter team lifespan limits the team members from developing a shared history or expectation to work together in the future. Authority differentiation refers to how decision-making roles are distributed across the team (Lee et al., 2015). Team members with high authority make decisions for the team in authority differentiated teams. Skills differentiation also plays a crucial role in determining team members with specialized knowledge and skills (Hollenbeck, Beersma, & Schouten, 2012). Such team members are difficult to substitute in a project. For the teams to perform well, members should depend on each other's knowledge and skills. At the same time, the fact that team members have specialized expertise limits the ability to assess their knowledge and contribution. The contribution to knowledge sharing enables team coordination and achieves a higher team performance (Smith-Jentsch et al., 2005). It was noted from the previous studies that knowledge sharing and coordination positively influence the dimensions of team social capital and team synergy (Srivastava et al., 2006; Zoltan, 2012).

2.4.1.4 Characteristics of Individual Team Members

Individual team members contribute to the dimensions of social capital and synergy by applying their work experiences, skills, and knowledge (Salas, Cooke, & Rosen, 2008). The characteristics of individual team members are related to their skills, psychological and their wellbeing (Patel, Pettitt, & Wilson, 2012). For team members to participate in software development and operations activities they need to be skilled in diverse methodologies, tools and techniques. The study of Acuna, Juristo, and Moreno (2006) found that the social dimension is as critical as technical capability. When team members work together with skills such as communicating and interacting with other team members, and stakeholders are necessary to coordinate task activities (Matturro, Raschetti, & Fontán, 2019). The existence of these skills contribute positively towards the dimensions of team social capital and team synergy.

Patel et al. (2012) described psychological factors as behavioral patterns that affects the way team members communicate, how they make decisions and contribute towards team effectiveness. They found that psychological characteristics of individual team members have an impact on team collaboration. Lacerenza, Marlow, Tannenbaum, and Salas (2018) also highlighted that when psychological safety exists, team members are more likely to discuss and share their views on software development and operations matters openly. Patel et al. (2012) stated that the physical and mental wellbeing of team members contributes towards collaborative work success. When individual team members start interacting with other team members, they build a sense of belonging to the team. Hence, influencing the dimensions of team social capital and team synergy.

2.4.1.5 Task Characteristics

Team members and teams engage in collaborative processes at work to accomplish tasks and fulfill their defined goals. Previous studies have identified these task characteristics (nature, structure, and demands of the task) as the primary attributes of the task that affect team synergy (Patel, Pettitt, & Wilson, 2012). The nature, structure and the demands of the task determine how complicated and correlated the task can be (Howard, Turban, & Hurley, 2016; Liu & Li, 2012), referred to as task interdependence. Task interdependence reflects the degree to which team members need to work together to perform well (De Jong et al., 2016).

2.4.1.6 Team Processes

Through team processes, team members engage and combine resources to perform and resolve the demands of their designated task activities. Therefore, the role of task processes is to mediate the relationship between inputs and outcomes of the task (Von Treuer, 2013). Team processes are dynamic in nature while they are described as a static phenomenon which may not represent the changes that exist in the variables that emerge over time as team members interact (Mathieu, Gilson, & Ruddy, 2006). Team processes are mutually dependent actions that transform inputs into outputs through cognitive, verbal, and behavioral activities focused on organizing taskwork to achieve common objectives (Costa, Passos, & Bakker, 2014). Team processes involve the interaction of team members with each other and with their task environment and are used to direct, align, and monitor what team members are doing. Being involved in team processes requires interaction, and the more team members interact, the more likely they are to develop team synergy. Leadership behavior, communication, cooperation, conflict resolution, and decision making are useful team processes that promote interaction among team members (Stock, 2004).

2.4.1.7 Use of Technology

Literature highlights that there are different views on the definition of technology (Carroll, 2017). For this study, technology refers to different software applications developed by people to provide means and methods to accomplish specific goals (Volti, 2009). The use of technology has assisted individuals and teams achieve their goals efficiently and effectively. Collaborative technologies are widely used to enable communication between collocated teams and dispersed teams. Technology can introduce a set of challenges that can impair the synergy between the team members. Limitations of the technology such as media quality, limited interactivity, and restrictions on the number of who can participate (Fenema, 2005). Use of technology may introduce fewer opportunities for face-to-face interactions and teams become less aware of a situation while depending too much on technology (Endsley & Jones, 2001).

2.4.1.8 Knowledge Sharing

Knowledge sharing is defined as "the provision or receipt of task information, know-how and feedback regarding a product or procedure" (Cummings, 2004, p. 352). In a project team, knowledge sharing is very important because it provides a link between the member and the project team by sharing knowledge to reduce cost and increase the performance. The literature highlights that a close relationship among team members (strong social ties) would increase contributors' willingness to share knowledge (Navimipour & Charband, 2016). Knowledge sharing provides an opportunity for collective learning to the teams, which leads to the generation of information and knowledge between the team. This will lead to the attainment of team synergy and constitute the components that embody team social capital (Zoltan, 2012).

2.4.2 Social Capital and Team Synergy

Social capital is essential for team collaboration and addresses the social and cultural prerequisites (Riemer and Klein 2008). Previous studies present that there are relationships between social capital and team synergy (Zoltan, 2012). Team synergy is defined as a phenomenon in which team members work together and influence the ability of the team to generate more and better solutions than the same people working as individuals (Zoltan, 2012; Glinow & McShare, 2010; Hackman, 1983). The final attribute of social capital is the creation of synergy (Tymon & Stumpf, 2003).

Social capital is defined as "the sum of the actual and potential resources embedded within, available through, and derived from the network of relationships possessed by an individual or social unit. Social capital thus comprises both the network and the assets that may be mobilized through that network" (Nahapiet and Ghoshal 1998, p. 243). It can be described in three dimensions namely: structural, cognitive, and relational dimensions. These dimensions can be applied as interconnected ties between team members (Nahapiet & Ghoshal, 1998; Wagner, Beimborn, & Weitzel, 2014). The structural dimension of social capital comprises of team cohesion and coordination (Zoltan, 2012). Structural ties portray the way team members interact. Coordination can happen physically by colocation, or virtually by emails (Liu et al., 2015). The cognitive dimension is defined as the assets that deliver shared understanding and meaning among the stakeholders (Lee, Park, & Lee 2013; Nahapiet and Ghoshal, 2000). This dimension comprises common language, shared codes, narratives, and perspectives as well as the team members' interpretation of reality (Wagner et al. 2014). The relational dimension embraces specific relationships that the people have, which are formed through trust, collaboration, relational norms and respect (Zoltan, 2012; Nahapiet & Ghoshal, 1998). The team members always view each other as partners and consult each other for better team synergy (Wagner et al. 2014).

2.5 Summary

In this chapter, the researcher examined existing literature on team synergy, team social capital, and the concept of DevOps in terms of the definition, principles, practices, and the challenges organizations and IT practitioners are facing in the adoption of DevOps. The purpose of this literature review was to show that the researcher is aware of existing studies and to position the research questions and objectives against the existing knowledge. Although the previous studies have identified various factors impacting software development teams, there are little to no studies to date sought to identify the factors that influence team synergy within software development teams.

This literature review has also revealed that there is a strong relationship between the dimensions of team social capital and team synergy. These concepts were helpful in choosing the theoretical framework for this research. It also helped the researcher to link these concepts with DevOps, where team collaboration plays a pivotal role and highly encouraged. Past studies focusing on DevOps discuss the concept in terms of its definition, principles, practices, and the challenges associated with its adoption. The researcher's current understanding of DevOps found in the literature enlightened the need to pursue this study and set the constructs that feed into the theoretical framework.

The review uncovered environmental factors, organizational factors, characteristics of the team, individual team members, the task characteristics, team processes, and knowledge sharing as the key factors that influence the synergy between development and IT operations in DevOps environment. The next chapter presents the research methodology, which explores the way the researcher will approach the data collection.

Chapter 3: Research Methodology

In this section, the researcher defines the research methodology and design that best suits and provide reasons for choosing it. Most importantly, the objective was to answer the research questions. Firstly, the researcher outlined the epistemological and theoretical grounding, followed by the research approach and methods for this study, and how these decisions anchored the research design and analysis process. Following that, it is a discussion of the sources used in the research setting, sampling design, data collection methods, and the analysis process. Finally, the section will conclude with a discussion of the strategies used to enhance the reliability and validity of the findings.

3.1 Philosophical Foundation

The philosophical assumptions underlying this research mainly encompass ontological and epistemological beliefs. Ontology refers to "the nature of our beliefs about reality" (Richards, 2003, p. 33). Ontological assumptions are concerned with what constitutes reality. These assumptions lead the researcher to inquire the form and nature of reality and what the researcher believes may be known about that reality. The existence of reality may be a singular, verifiable reality, and truth or socially constructed multiple realities (Patton, 2002). In this study, the researcher's position regarding the perceptions about the nature of reality follows a relativist ontology. A relativist ontology suggests that there are multiple realities (Duncan & Lincoln, 2005). Epistemology refers to assumptions about the knowledge on the subject under investigation, and it may be constructed, acquired, and communicated (Myers, 1997).

The epistemology composing this qualitative research is in the form of constructivism. This approach supports that individuals seek and create meaning in different ways, even when experiencing the same situation (Crotty, 1998). The literature identifies several assumptions of constructivism (Neuman, 2013; Lincoln, Lynham, & Guba, 2011; Crotty, 1998), three of which are key to this study: meaning is built by people as they engage with the world they are interpreting, therefore qualitative researchers incline to use open-ended questions, so that the participants can share their perspectives; people interact with their world and make sense of it based on their historical and social orientation; and the basic creation of meaning is always social, arising in and out of interaction with a human community, in this case, software development teams and stakeholders. Therefore, the research meaning and conclusions in qualitative research are context specific.

Constructivism is very useful as the philosophical stance for this study following Stake's revelation on the importance of a qualitative researcher playing a dual role, being the gatherer and the interpreter, to nurture the belief that knowledge is created rather than discovered (Stake, 1995).This study aims at identifying and interpreting the factors that influence team synergy between development and IT operations in a DevOps environment. The aim is to understand how the behaviors, interactions, and roles of software developers and operations personnel support team synergy.

3.2 Research Approach

Research approaches are used for building or testing theories, and Bhattacherjee (2012) identified two main approaches as deductive and inductive. This study adopts a deductive approach to theory as it begins by identifying a theoretical framework based on the existing literature accompanied by data collection, where the data will be interpreted to create meaning based on the context of the theoretical framework (Saunders, Lewis, & Thornhill, 2009). In a deductive approach, the researcher uses theory deductively and put it upfront as the beginning of a study (Bahari, 2010). The theory used in the study becomes a framework throughout the entire study, organizing model for the research questions and procedures for data collection (Creswell, 2003). Likewise, Zoltan's theoretical framework for team social capital as a basis for organizational team synergy (discussed in Section 2.4) was applied and tested in this study.

3.3 Research Design

This section presents a detailed plan for data collection, which aims to respond to a set of research questions. The processes suggested by Bhattacherjee (2012) consist of the sampling process, instrument development process, data collection process, and data analysis. In this study, a comprehensive literature review was conducted to identify the factors that might influence the synergy between development and IT operations in a DevOps environment according to literature. Following the nature and scope of the study, a qualitative study was conducted to address the research questions in the form of a case study.

- **Case Study**

A case study is a detailed inquiry of a problem that may exist in one or more real-world settings over an extended period (Creswell, 2014). Cases are time and activity bound, and researchers collect specific information using a mixture of data collection procedures over a sustained period (Stake, 1995; Yin, 2009, 2012; Bhattacherjee, 2012). There are different types of case studies, which were classified by Baxter and Jack (2008) as descriptive, intrinsic explanatory, exploratory, instrumental, collectives and multiple case studies. The focus of this research is to adopt an exploratory single case study. According to Siggelkow (2007), a single case study can describe in detail the existence of the subject matter. It is better to perform a single case study when the researcher requires to study a group of people (Yin, 2003). He also revealed that a single case study with embedded units can be performed if the researcher desires to have the capability to study the case with data analysis within data analyses, therefore the researcher can have the opportunity to explore the subunits that are embedded within the larger cases (Gustafsson, 2017).

Case study researchers collect specific information using a mixture of data collection procedures over a sustained period. In this case, the researcher will collect data using observations, semi-structured interviews, and review of documents that will be provided by the software project teams where the study is carried out. The case study should incorporate the research questions, the purpose of the study, the unit of analysis and criteria for evaluating findings (Yin, 2009). The most appropriate questions for this type of qualitative case study research are "how" and "what" forms of questions and this study deals with the "what" factors influence the synergy between development and IT operations. Furthermore, it identifies the "what" factors promotes or prevents the synergy between the development and IT operations. The study's units of analysis will be the sampled DevOps software projects selected from the participating organization and the project teams (development and operations) involved. The theoretical framework that links data to the intentions of the study will guide the data collection process. The researcher will analyze the data to match the patterns that appear in the data to the theoretical propositions of the case study. During the development of the subject matter, the researcher will extract the meaning from the findings and determine recommendations for the discipline and future studies.

The purpose of this study explored the factors that influence the synergy between software development and IT operations in a DevOps environment. The study also described the importance of team synergy in promoting team effectiveness and performance in DevOps environments. Furthermore, the study sought to understand the attitudes and experiences of DevOps teams, and in turn, identify conditions that promote a positive team synergy. A case study was found appropriate in this situation, where the researcher, as well as practitioners, search for new insights (Eisenhardt, 1989). The researcher conducted this case study in a real work environment, where new findings and a broader understanding of the topic were achieved.

3.4 Case Description

3.4.1 Case Organisation

The study took place at TOrg, one of South Africa's leading information and communication technology services provider. TOrg provides communication services for mobile, home and business. The organization was established in 1991, and it operates in all the nine provinces in South Africa. It also operates in 38 African countries from its regional operation hubs in Kenya and Nigeria. The organisation grew from the time when telecommunications infrastructure was split from the Department of Posts and Telecommunications. TOrg's product offerings consist of ADSL, Fibre, Wireless broadband and mobile internet services. In 2018, the organization had a total of 18 286 employees.

TOrg is structured is to have a retail, wholesale, networks, information and communication technology (ICT), marketing and advertising and infrastructure divisions. The retail division, also known as the consumer division, provides both fixed and mobile broadband services as well as voice technology. The wholesale division focusses on small to medium business enterprises and includes data and voice connectivity, information technology services and marketing services. Networks divisions focus on connectivity and has successfully built and run high-speed broadband networks that links banking systems, hospitals and schools. Advertising and Marketing provides commercial search solutions and integrated, effective advertising and marketing, especially for Small to Medium Enterprises (SME) businesses. The infrastructure division, for provides masts and towers solutions, property management services and property development. The ICT division provides converged ICT solutions and end-to-end digital solutions for enterprise customers.

3.4.2 The Role of IT at TOrg

TOrg sees IT as a business enabler, which provides an end-to-end digital solution and allows the business to respond rapidly to market changes. Thus, there is a higher expenditure on IT each year, as part of TOrg's drive towards digital transformation, which requires infrastructure upgrades, and funding on software development projects. The software development projects are carried out by in-house staff and outsourced staff. TOrg develops and maintains its suite of software applications, typically Operations Support Systems (OSS) and Business Support Systems (BSS). These applications are designed to support the business and services offered by TOrg. The software development teams continually align TOrg business with IT and ensure the IT systems adapts to the changing business environment and remain supportive of the core business. Although the teams knew the significance of IT to the business, they were striving to deliver the required business value. Most of the problems experienced were because of the disconnection between the development and operations teams. All these problems experienced triggered the need for a more reliable software development approach.

Before the adoption of DevOps, agility, reliability and team collaboration were major problems at TOrg, which negatively affected the quality of the systems that were delivered. Defects were regularly injected into the production environment, causing instability to the production environment. Reliability can be described as the possibility that the system will perform its intended function sufficiently without failure. The poor quality of software delivery resulted in a loss of customer satisfaction and growing tension between the development and operations teams. The IT division was not fulfilling the business needs, and hence it was regarded as being unreliable and costly. Therefore, TOrg business units questioned the effectiveness of IT. These were the problems that prompted IT to search for new methods of software development.

3.4.3 Background of DevOps at TOrg

In the move to improve agility, team collaboration and reliability of the software delivery, TOrg introduced the Agile methodology to its software development teams in 2010. That was a shift from the traditional waterfall methodology. The idea behind was to have speed in the delivery of software to cope with rising demands from the business. However, the approach did not make much of difference regarding speed and reliability of software delivery. The Agile teams were operating, mainly at development and testing phase without involving operations team members.

In 2017, through new management, Torg decided to use a different approach. The new approach was intended to address the collaboration and communication barriers that were facing the IT department. The drive to adopt DevOps within TOrg was aimed at improving team collaboration between the development and operations teams. The continuous integration and continuous delivery aspect of DevOps were seen as a key driver of faster releases at Torg. As part of the DevOps implementation strategy, the management selected a project team and a target release, in which development teams and operations teams were all involved from the inception of the targeted release. At first, the development and operations teams were not sure of their roles and responsibilities in the new approach. The outcome of the release was not pleasing as there was no clarity as to who should perform what tasks. Also, both teams trying to adjust from their old silo tendencies. As result, the targeted release was regarded as unsuccessful.

TOrg management began to engage with other role players in the industry, who have successfully adopted DevOps. It prompted the organisation to bring external DevOps specialists to guide the development and operations teams. The specialists also provided in-house training to the teams to speed up the adoption process. The first attempt failed because the development and operations had no one to guide them, also because of limited knowledge on the approach. The adoption of DevOps was successful after going for DevOps training and the involvement of external DevOps specialists who guided the team during the process of implementation. TOrg then decided to embrace DevOps as the *de facto* standard for all its development teams.

3.4.4 The Software Development Teams

TOrg consists of diverse and cross-functional software development teams, consisting of both development and IT operations combined, that is DevOps teams. These teams work on multiple projects within a multi-tiered development environment. A span of technologies and software development languages are used to support the software development process. Team members are selected and assigned to software projects based on skills required by the project. A single project may consist of a team of 12 to 15 active members. Usually, these teams are structured based on the section of the system they are working on, although they all commit their work to a single repository. The organization's integrated multi-tiered development environment allows multiple development teams to work concurrently, from different geographic locations and commit their work to a single centralized repository.

3.4.5 Research Site

The thirteen participants were all from Cape Town office. There were no issues gaining access to the research location or barriers in finding an appropriate site to perform this study. Formal arrangements with the responsible organization and tiers of management were made in advance. The researcher launched a formal request (see Appendix A) to the participating organization for permission to perform the study at their premises.

3.5 Sampling Technique

According to Neuman (2013), sampling is a method of selecting cases to carry out a detailed inquiry, so that the researcher can learn and understand the phenomenon under investigation. Onwuegbuzie and Leech (2007) classified sampling schemes as either probability or non-probability. The different types of non-probability are snowballing, purposive, quota, and convenience (Neuman, 2010). This research used qualitative data, which provided the researcher freedom to use their own discretion during data analysis (Onwuegbuzie & Leech, 2007). In particular, non-probability purposive sampling was used to select the thirteen participants who were interviewed in this research. The participants and situations were selected based on their relevance to the study, knowledge and their experience working in DevOps environments.

In quantitative research, the researcher follows a standard procedure and a random selection of participants to isolate a probable influence of external variables and ensure the generalizability of results while in qualitative research purposive sampling is used to select the subject (Sargeant, 2012; Palinkas et al., 2013). The thirteen participants (see table) were chosen based on who can best inform the research questions and further improve understanding of the phenomenon under study.

Table 3.1: List of Participants

Name	Role	Team
LC	Domain Lead	A
MM	Senior Developer / Principal Developer	A

TT	SharePoint / .Net Developer	A
SK	Senior Java Consultant	A
AL	Senior Systems Analyst	B
NP	Acting Senior Manager	B, C
NA	Business Support Manager	B
DJ	Dev Database Administrator	B
MS	Systems Analyst	B
RH	Systems Administration & Application support	B
BB	Senior Ops Database Administrator	C
JA	Dev Specialist/ Development Team lead	C
LS	Systems Analyst/Developer	C

3.6 Data Collection

The following will be discussed in the data collection section: the data collection methods employed and the timeframe of the study. These are important elements needed to conduct a comprehensive data collection (Rowlands, 2005).

Bhattacherjee (2012) argues that qualitative methods like case studies depend mostly on non-numeric data, unlike quantitative approaches that are concerned with numeric data. In a case study, it is necessary to merge data sources, also referred to as triangulation. Triangulation is crucial to ensure the reliability of the case study (Yin, 2009). Supplementary data sources of data facilitate case study researchers to create a chain of evidence and robustness (Runeson, Host, Rainer, & Regnell, 2012). Therefore, this study employed interviewing as the primary data collection method in conjunction with participant observation and document review.

3.6.1 Interviews

Interviews are one of the most common qualitative methods designed to acquire a clear perspective of the participant's experiences, views, and feelings on the research topic. The researcher's interviewing methods remain motivated by the desire to understand everything the participant can share about the subject (Mack et al., 2005).

Interviewing (semi-structured) was used as the principal data source for this study for the following the reasons highlighted in the literature (Edwards & Holland, 2013; Patton, 2002; Merriam, 2002). These are 1). to explore people's understandings of their lives and aspects of their experiences 2). to discover what is in the participant's mind and things that cannot be observed directly, such as feelings, thoughts, and intentions 3). to create descriptions of the subject matter allowing readers to make decisions about the application of the study results.

For this study, the selected team members from ongoing DevOps software projects were interviewed. The selected team members were interviewed face-to-face to a point when the researcher reached saturation point. In total, thirteen participants were selected for the interviews based their availability and willingness. As highlighted in the literature, when using purposive sampling, the population sample is based on theoretical saturation, described as the point where new data no longer bring additional insights to the research question (Mark et al., 2005). Interviewing key team members from each project team helped to establish and elicit data from participants who are actively involved and could share their experiences, opinions, and knowledge about the research questions fluently. The interviews took place between the 5th February 2019 and the 7th of June 2019. The duration of the interviews was approximately 45 minutes to 1 hour. The researcher conducted face-to-face interviews at the research site. The interviews were recorded to ensure accurate transcription. The researcher also made handwritten notes during each interview to keep track of the key points and to highlight important ideas. The interview questions (see Appendix B) were formulated based on the theoretical framework.

3.6.2 Participant Observation

During participant observation, data was collected by observing the participants' behaviors, events, interactions, and processes as they occur in their natural setting. It requires the researcher to be present at, involved in, and recording the routine daily activities with the software development and IT operations team members. The literature highlights that participant observation emerged from traditional ethnographic studies (Mack et al., 2005).

While observing the participants perform their tasks and during design review sessions and daily standup meetings, the researcher made careful, objective notes on what was realized, recorded all activities and observations as notes. The researcher observed how the development and operations team members interacted during meetings, design review sessions and when they performed their daily work activities and took note of any characteristics that could influence to the synergy of the teams. Through participant observation, the researcher initiated open discussions with DevOps team members and captured as much information as possible. An observation report (see Appendix C) was compiled using the information and messages captured

3.6.3 Document Review

Although interviews and participant observation were the primary methods of data collection, data was also collected by reviewing documents. The types of documents that were reviewed were from the selected projects. The documents include functional design specifications documents, technical specifications documents, deployment submission documents, and other documents related to activities involving DevOps teams. Document review is useful to clarify or substantiate participants' statements (Yin, 2013), and to provide a thick description of the case (Esterberg, 2002; Merriam, 2002). The document review process was useful in providing information that helped the researcher to support the monitoring and evaluation of data collection activities. It also assisted software development and IT operations personnel to identify critical issues could be addressed and gave a better understanding of how the synergy between development and IT operations personnel is achieved.

3.7. Data Analysis

The study derived the general constructs for social capital as well as the factors that leverage team synergy. Thematic coding was to investigate the factors that influence the synergy between development and IT operations. Thematic coding is very useful when the researcher aims to identify categories and examine their relationships (Runyan, Huddleston, & Swinney, 2007; Sarker, Xiao, & Beaulieu, 2013).

The principal purpose of data interpretation is, as in any other analysis, to derive conclusions from the data, keeping a clear chain of evidence (Runeson et al., 2012). Creswell (2009) recommends that before deciding on an appropriate technique, the researcher should select a potential data analysis method based on the intentions of the study. The motivation of this study was a discovery need, where the researcher sought to identify the factors that influence the synergy between development and IT operations in a DevOps environment. The method of data analysis used to analyze the qualitative data for this investigation is a thematic analysis technique (Braun & Clarke, 2006).

Thematic analysis method essentially research for emerging themes that arise as being critical when describing the subject matter or phenomenon (Fereday & Muir-Cochrane, 2006). Themes are recurring and distinguishing features manifesting the feelings and experiences of the team members (King & Horrocks, 2011). Data collected from the interviews was recorded into audio files, then transferred into transcripts using Nvivo software. Next, this study adopted a six-phase thematic analysis (see Table 3.2) to analyse the transcribed data.

Table 3:2: Phases of Thematic Analysis (Adapted from Braun and Clarke, 2006)

Phase	Description of Phase
1. Familiarising with data	Transcribe and read over data
2. Generating initial codes	Generate codebook after re-reading data.
3. Searching for themes	Combine codes into potential themes
4. Reviewing themes	Compare themes against each other and the entire data set
5. Defining and naming themes	Name themes so as to create a story effect
6. Producing the report	Produce a succinct and interest report of results, which are related back to research questions and literature

3.7.1 Familiarising with data

The first step involves starting to identify, and record, potentially interesting features of the data, relevant to the research question (Braun & Clarke). For the researcher, it is an act of transcribing data, becoming familiar with the data, and finding patterns that aid the creation of meaning. Familiarisation of the data is followed by the process of systematically coding the data to generate initial codes.

3.7.2 Generating initial codes

A code represents a succinct label that captures something interesting about the data (Charmaz, 2006). The aim of the researcher here is to identify potentially meaningful portions of the data at the smallest level (Boyatzis, 1998). This step involves noting interesting features and appropriate data that are categorized into important groups. This phase ends with the compilation of a list of the codes, and collation of all the data relevant to each code. Figure 3.8 shows an example of a code generated from transcribed data.

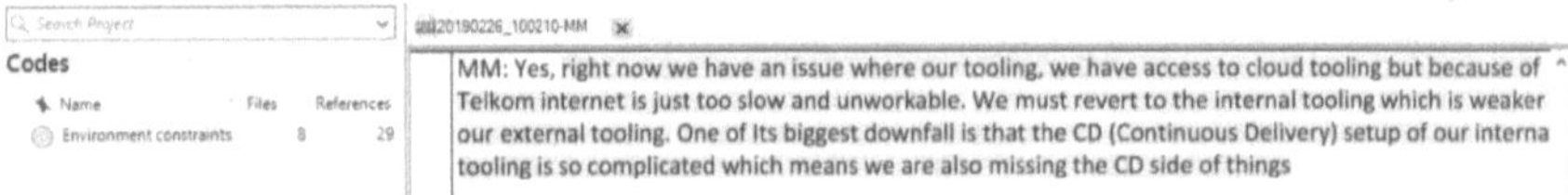

Figure 3.8: Generating Codes from Transcribed Data

3.7.3 Searching for themes

A theme identifies a meaning formed across the dataset, which is important for illuminating the research question (Braun & Clarke, 2006). In this phase different codes were organised into possible themes. In addition, the appropriate coded data extracts within the identified themes were organised. According to Braun and Clarke, in the deductive case, themes must relate to constructs in a pre-existing theoretical framework. Since this study adopted a deductive approach, the themes are associated to the constructs of the theoretical framework. The relationship between the themes and the constructs of the theoretical framework is presented in Table 3.8. This phase ends with a set of candidate themes, which are outlined in the form of a thematic map, and the relationship of the coded data relevant to each theme.

Table 3.8: Relationship of Analysed Data to Theoretical Framework

FACTORS	Structural			Relational				Cognitive			
Environmental	TC	CO	EN	TR	CB	NO	RS	CL	SC	SN	SP
Technical Constraints	√	√	√	√	√	√	√	√	√	√	√
Social Constraints	√	√	√	√	√	√	√	√	√	√	√
Organisational											
Management Support	√	√	√	√	√	√	√	√	√	√	√
Functional Boundaries	√	√	√	√	√	√		√	√	√	√
Regulatory Processes	√	√	√	√	√	√	√	√	√	√	√
Organisation Restructuring	√	√	√	√	√	√	√	√	√	√	√
Organisation Culture	√	√	√	√	√	√	√	√	√	√	√
Task Characteristics											
Nature of Work	√	√	√	√	√	√	√	√	√	√	√
Good Management of Task Dependencies	√	√	√	√	√	√	√	√	√	√	√
Team Characteristics											
Skills differentiation	√	√	√	√	√	√	√	√	√	√	√
Member Characteristics											
Social Skills	√	√	√	√	√	√	√	√	√	√	√
Mentoring Skills	√	√	√	√	√	√	√	√	√	√	√
Team Engagement Skills	√	√	√	√	√	√	√	√	√	√	√
Team Processes											
Leadership Behaviour	√	√	√	√	√	√	√	√	√	√	√
Decision-making	√	√	√	√	√	√	√	√	√	√	√
Use of Technology											
Choice of Technology	√	√	√	√	√	√	√	√	√	√	√
Challenges of Using Technology	√	√	√	√	√	√	√	√	√	√	√
Knowledge Sharing											
Information shared	√	√	√	√	√	√	√	√	√	√	√
Willingness to Share Information	√	√	√	√	√	√	√	√	√	√	√

Key	
TC	Team Cohesion
CO	Coordination
EN	Engagement
TR	Trust
CB	Collaboration
NO	Norms
RS	Respect
CL	Common Language
SC	Shared Codes
SN	Shared Narratives
SP	Shared Perspectives

3.7.4 Reviewing themes

Throughout the reviewing process, the researcher checks that each theme is consistent and substantial, with clear boundaries and a distinct central organizing concept. Potential themes are refined, coherent patterns are organized to form a thematic map, and themes and coded quotations are reviewed to identify if a relationship exists. The researcher ends this phase with a final set of themes.

3.7.5 Defining and naming themes

In this phase, the researcher selects the data extracts to be used in the final report and develops and builds the analysis into its final form, with each theme addressing the research question. One of the crucial parts of this stage is naming each theme and ensure the names are informative and engaging, for instance, short data quotes that capture the meaning of the theme can be used (Braun & Clarke, 2006).

3.7.6 Producing the report

This phase provides the final opportunity for refining the analysis, such as through the integration of literature, or determining the order in which the themes are to be presented (Braun & Clarke, 2006). A concise, coherent and logical final analysis, with data extracts that demonstrate the commonness of the theme, are combined into an argument that relates to the research question. Finally, a report is produced.

3.8 Reliability and Validity

Qualitative methodology approaches differently to the validity and reliability of the knowledge produced in research (Merriam, 1998). Case study researchers need to guarantee construct validity (through the triangulation of multiple sources of evidence, chains of evidence, and member checking), internal validity (using established analytic techniques such as pattern matching), external validity (through analytic generalization), and reliability (through case study protocols and databases (Yin, 2002).

3.8.1 Construct Validity

Construct validity refers to the degree to which a study investigates what it claims to examine that is to the extent to which a method leads to an accurate view of reality (Denzin & Lincoln, 1994). It is concerned with revealing and overcoming subjectivity, by linking data collection questions and measures to research questions and suggestions (Rowley, 2002). Yin (1994) stated that case study researchers sometimes do not develop a well-thought set of measures, and instead, they use their individual experiences. However, he urged researchers to establish a more transparent chain of evidence and use different data collection methods and multiple data sources. Construct validity is reinforced by the use of various sources of evidence, and these multiple sources of evidence can include multiple viewpoints within and across the data sources (Meyer, 2001). This study responded to these requirements in its sampling of interviewees and the use of multiple data sources. Data was collected by interviewing and observing the participants as well as reviewing documents.

3.8.2 Internal validity

Internal validity in qualitative research deals with the credibility of findings, and how related the conclusions are to the real world. Internal validity is usually exhibited in the analysis stage (Yin, 1994). In this study, thematic analysis was used to ensure internal validity, making sure that the concepts that were reported on, occurred across multiple interviews (Shenton, 2004). A description of how the analysis process was conducted to achieve internal validity was provided in section 3.8.

3.8.3 External validity

External validity in qualitative research refers to transferability of findings, which is the extent to which they can be applied to other settings (Shenton, 2004). To ensure this, purposive sampling was used (Anfara, Brown, & Mangione, 2002) and a rich description of the results was done with many direct quotations included (Myers & Newman, 2007).

3.8.4 Reliability

Reliability in qualitative research refers to dependability of the research, which is the extent to which the study can be repeated by other researchers (Shenton, 2004). Reliability will be assured in the following ways. An audit trail was used (Anfara et al., 2002) by the researcher through documenting all activities, data collection chronology and data analysis procedures comprehensively (Creswell and Miller, 2000).

The use of triangulation as mentioned in the construct validity section also enhances the reliability of the research (Anfara et al., 2002). Also, to help other researchers to depend on the findings, the effectiveness of the study is demonstrated in the discussion and limitations sections (Shenton, 2004).

3.8.5 Objectivity

Objectivity in qualitative research refers to the confirmability of the research, which entails ensuring as far as possible that the findings emerge from participants' experiences and ideas, instead of the researcher's preferences (Shenton, 2004). This was achieved mainly through multiple information sources being asked the same questions, like using software developers

through to operations personnel (data triangulation) and constant practice reflexivity (Anfara et al., 2002). To be reflexive is to be self-aware. So, the researcher was always conscious of influencing the research. For instance, when coding interviews, it was not just based on the researcher's thoughts but also on the literature (Finlay, 2002). Likewise, even the audit trail/clear description of the research process mentioned in reliability section adds to the confirmability of the research as others can check exactly how data were gathered. Furthermore, the researcher has stated underlying philosophical beliefs and assumptions which underpin the research, giving further transparency. Finally, confirmability is also shown in the admission of the research's limitations at the end of this paper (Shenton, 2004).

3.9 Ethical Considerations

The emphasis of this study is to identify the factors that influence the synergy between development and operations teams within a DevOps environment. We are required to obey the organization's confidentiality policy. Therefore, data collected through recommended methods will be protected by a nondisclosure agreement. For that reason, the names to be used in the study will be adjusted to protect the identity of the organization and those participating.

The study adopts the principles of ethical considerations that were compiled by Bryman and Bell (2007) as essential guidelines. These include:

- The study will assure that research participants will not be subjected to harm in any ways whatsoever. We will avoid the use of offensive, discriminating, or other unacceptable languages in the suggested data collection methods.

- A letter (presented in Appendix D) requesting to obtain the participants' full consent will be sent to each participant before the study commences. Accordingly, the respondents will participate in the study voluntarily.

- The interview questions will be made available to the UCT Ethics Committee for review and approval.

- A completed ethics application form will be made available to the UCT Ethics Committee for approval.

- The study will assure that there is an adequate level of privacy and confidentiality of the research data. We understand that our trust and honor will be at risk if we fail to keep our promise on confidentiality. We will keep all audio records and transcripts encrypted. The study will also remove the real names of interviewees from the transcripts before data analysis.

- We ensure the anonymity of individuals and organizations participating in the research.

- The research will eliminate any pretense or misrepresentation of the purpose and objective of the study.

- Declaration of affiliations in any forms, sources of funding, as well as any possible conflicts of interests.

- The study will avoid the use of misleading information or any bias in the representation of the findings.

Chapter 4: Research Findings

This chapter presents the research findings which are derived from the analysis of semi structured interviews, document reviews and participant observations. The following research questions informed this study:

(1) What are the factors that influence the synergy between software development and IT operations teams in a DevOps environment?

(2) What factors are enablers of relational, structural and cognitive dimensions of social capital as a basis for team synergy between development and IT operations teams?

(3) What factors are inhibitors of relational, structural and cognitive dimensions of social capital as a basis for team synergy between development and IT operations teams?

During the analysis of the transcribed data, themes and categories were identified. The themes and categories that emerged from the data sources were aligned to the theoretical framework.

4.1 Environmental Factors

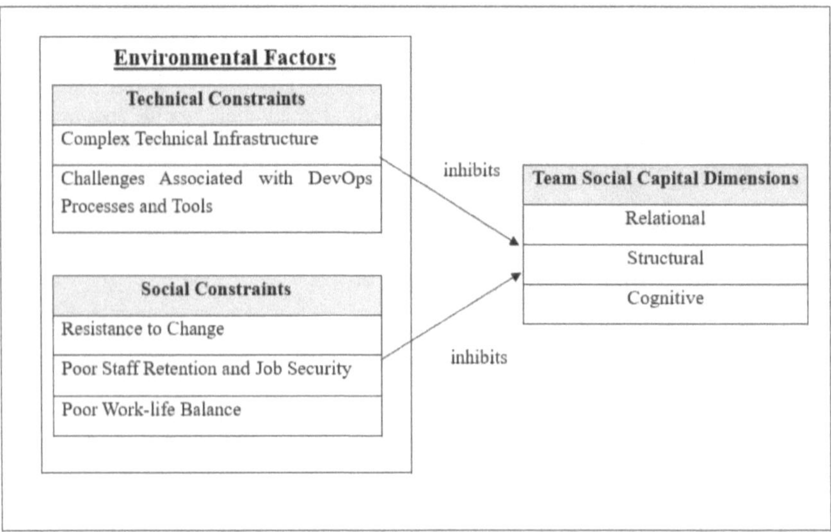

Figure 4.1: Environmental Factors

According to Patel, Pettitt and Wilson (2012), an environment consists of the physical space, socio-cultural aspects of the workplace and the work organisation that individuals and teams operate in. In this study, this definition is extended to include that of Todino, Viglietti, Tranchero and de Juan-Marin (2016), who described environment as a set of consolidated tools designed to support various activities of the software development process. Figure 4.1 depict the environmental factors that inhibit team social capital as basis for team synergy. The study did not identify environmental factors that promote the dimensions of team social capital.

4.1.1 Technical Constraints

Technical constraints refer to technical aspects of a particular process or tool that negatively affects team productivity. These aspects mostly arise from the teams as well as their work environment (Riungu-Kalliosaari, Mäkinen, Lwakatare, Tiihonen, & Männistö, 2016). The participants described technical constraints in terms of the complex technical infrastructure and challenges associated with DevOps processes and tools.

4.1.1.1 Complex Technical Infrastructure

Infrastructure refers to the software architecture, software support tools, language engineering platforms, and development environment needed to operate an application service or system (Cunningham, Humphreys, Gaizauskas, & Wilks, 1997). The infrastructure is continuously evolving and becoming sophisticated as a result of scaling DevOps patterns to the cloud and the increasing demand for automation (Cukier, 2013; Sandobalin, Insfran, & Abrahao, 2017). The participants indicated that the complex technical infrastructure introduces challenges that affect relationships among the DevOps teams. As a result, it impairs the team social capital dimensions, which creates the foundation of team synergy.

According to TT, *"the major constraint is probably the technology itself because most people in my team have no experience and they are still figuring out how the Azure DevOps deployment process works"*. In addition, MM stated that, *"one of its biggest downfalls is that the Continuous Integration/Continuous Deployment (CI/CD) setup of our internal tooling is so complicated which means we are also missing the CD side of things"*. The infrastructure requires more processing power and more machines to the resources pool, for platforms to connect to intertwined microservices, which makes the internal CI/CD setup complex and riddled with problems. Furthermore, MM explained that, *"team members are sent on a 4-day training session which is completely insufficient. So, it is very difficult to start up a DevOps environment when people are not on same page due to lack of knowledge on the subject."* It is difficult for the development and operations teams to work together when team members are not on the same page. The participants also found that team members struggle to know and implement all the services due to limited skills and knowledge on the subject, *"resulting in more self-inflicted constraints: Time-consuming, unnecessary de-bugging of environments, e.g. Uniform Resource Locators (URLs) pointing to the incorrect environment, settings that change between deployments or environment initialization" [AL].* A lot of time is lost with DevOps team members trying to make sense of the technical infrastructure, which leads to poor coordination of tasks and limited sharing of task-related information and knowledge between development and operations. *"Technically, it gets quite complex in terms of trying to get to the target server to access and perform DevOps work because the target server is deeply hidden in the network." [BB]. "The complex infrastructure makes development, integration, as well as preparation and deployments extremely complex and riddled with problems." [AL]* Poor coordination and limited knowledge sharing prevent the structural and cognitive dimensions of team social capital. The participants felt that a lack of knowledge sharing and lack of coordination prevents team collaboration between development and operations. Therefore, it hurts the structural, relational and cognitive dimensions of team social capital.

4.1.1.2 Challenges Associated with DevOps Processes and Tools

Past studies acknowledge that DevOps teams utilize various tools to continuously integrate and deploy software, and enforce processes that encourage team collaboration (Bass, Weber, & Zhu, 2015; Erich, Amrit, & Daneva, 2017). The participants described the following technical constraints in relation to the challenges associated with DevOps processes and tools: (1) expired licenses and service plan, and storage space issues, and (2) limited support for DevOps practices, and (3) counter-productive processes.

- **Expired Licenses and Service Plan, and Storage Space issues**

The participants felt that the challenges they encounter with processes and tools impair the relational, structural and cognitive dimensions of social capital, preventing them from achieving team synergy, resulting in their DevOps teams to be not as productive as desired. LC, a Domain Lead for Intranet and Online Channels, stated that, *"... the environment and the use of technology are the biggest stumbling blocks that we have currently, for example, end of licensing and space issues. We end up running on outdated technologies".* She revealed that some of the proprietary DevOps tools have different licensing plans, which are renewed at designated periods. The participants indicated that they have to use outdated tools when some of the licensing requirements are far too expensive to accommodate all the development and operations personnel. Thus, the development and IT operations teams are incapable of accomplishing their work collaboratively whilst using the same tools. As a result, it is challenging for them to collaborate and coordinate their development and deployment activities as a unified team.

The constraint associated to expired licenses and service plan inhibit structural and relational dimensions of team social capital. The participants explained that when the licenses for these tools expire, team members risk using unsupported versions or not being able to use these tools. *"Some of our DevOps tools are not supported by the vendors anymore. We are not receiving updates and hotfixes for these tools because the licenses expired. Team members are demotivated and restricted in their capabilities to provide solutions and perform their tasks efficiently." [LC].* The teams cannot coordinate their interdependent tasks effectively when DevOps processes fail because of tools that have unexpectedly reached it end of life or end of license. The teams' social cohesion is negatively affected by minimizing the pace at which development and operations team members interact, communicate, and share their tasks, undermining the structural dimension of team social capital.

Furthermore, the participants pointed out that they encounter challenges related to lack of storage capacity: *"not enough space on the disk" [MM].* According to the participants, these challenges are frequently encountered when files generated from the build process exceed the storage capacity provided by the DevOps plan. The participants noted that these introduce delays in the DevOps integration and deployment processes. Development and IT operations team members are frustrated because they cannot continue with their work and are under pressure from the other teams waiting for the build and deployment process to complete. *"Running out of storage space interrupts continuous deployment services and the flow of work between development and operations. Our builds and production deployment cannot proceed. The build process hangs, or it does not start at all." [MM].* The participants explained that end of licensing and space issues create obstacles to the interaction between development and IT operations, therefore limiting the exchange of information, task related ideas, and knowledge between the team members. As a result, it prevents the cognitive dimension of team social capital.

- **Limited Support for DevOps Practices**

The second challenge relates to the use of tools that offer limited support for DevOps practices. The participants mentioned tools such as ClearCase, Harvest, Enterprise Architecture, etc. ClearCase and Harvest are code repository and versioning tools. They suggested that such tools should have comprehensive build and automation mechanisms to support DevOps processes effectively. According to LS, *"It's very much manual work where you would normally expect your versioning tool to be automatically integrated into your development toolsets."* It reveals that the tools are missing the essential features needed to support DevOps automated build operations. Appropriate DevOps continuous integration and deployment tools allow development and operations teams to perform automated builds, deployments and monitoring to eliminate inherent problems that are likely to emerge during the deployment process, if manually driven. The participants mentioned that there is a high risk of human errors when the process is manual. Therefore, there are no guarantees of deploying safe code to the production environment, which may result in IT operations team members blame the development team for introducing bugs in the production environment. The level of trust between the two teams is negatively affected, which leads to the impaired relational dimension of team social capital.

According to MS, *"We don't use tools specifically for running a good DevOps process, which is what I found lacking from the time I started working here. I come from an environment where we had good DevOps tools to help us manage projects. It generally means it takes a lot longer to achieve we want to achieve because the collaboration in not all round since some people are not actively involved. It makes the process stagnant at some point because some information might not be readily available."* The participant highlights that the tools that they use limited when it comes to the support of DevOps practices, making it difficult for the development and IT operations teams to achieve the desired team collaboration and knowledge sharing, which potentially impairs the relational and cognitive dimensions of team social capital.

- **Counter-productive processes**

The third challenge relates to counter-productive processes. Most of the participants reported that the processes in place are integrated ITIL (Information Technology Infrastructure Library) processes with DevOps. They reported that the change management style associated with ITIL is not adapted for DevOps teams as it is commonly associated with long administrative and silo driven processes. LC described it as, *"the current environment prevents team synergy from progressing to where we want it to be, it creates additional blockages"*. It takes a long time to implement change requests due to the change control process. As a result, there is less team engagement and collaboration between the development and operations teams. According to the participants, the process involves presenting the change requests to the Change Advisory Board (CAB) for approval, later followed by Change Order (CO) to deploy the changes. No matter how simple or small the change is, it has to go through the same process. The participants felt that these CAB meetings are a waste of time since they are characterised by poor attendance and are sometimes only for rubber-stamping. The processes are *"outdated and counter-productive, were put in place years ago by another large organisation as part of the organisation's need to implement IT corporate governance"* [AL] It is therefore difficult to manage DevOps projects on such an environment. For that reason, DevOps teams feel continuously drawn backwards in their joint efforts to deliver changes rapidly, resulting in low morale and less collaboration. *"Operations team members feel that they are not always provided the necessary resources (tools, training, etc.) when a deployment is done, but the development team feels that the operations team does not contribute valuable input when they have the opportunity"* [AL]. Low morale gives rise to a lack of team cohesion and a lack of trust among team members, which prevents the engagement of development and IT operations teams. Therefore, the structural and relational dimensions of team social capital are negatively affected by low morale, lack of team collaboration, and lack of team cohesion.

4.1.2 Social Constraints

Social constraints are driven by human-related aspects of the software development process. Sanchez-Gordón, Colomo-Palacios, and Herranz (2016) defined human factors as characteristics of a person that affect performance and learning. These includes a person's social behavior and cognitive characteristics, essential to build team social capital dimensions. The following themes relating to human factors were identified from the data: (1) resistance to change, (2) poor staff retention and job security, and (3) poor work-life balance.

4.1.2.1 Resistance to Change

Resistance to change is described as any conduct in line with attempting to maintain the status quo and as persistence in avoiding change (Pardo del Val & Martínez Fuentes, 2003; Kim & Lee, 2016). It has been noted that most people are resistant to change at some level, but resistance is highly influenced by an individual's interests, tolerance and experience (Hon, Bloom, & Crant, 2014).

The participants revealed that some are resistant to change because they believe that the changes are disruptive and are likely to introduce uncertainties to a stable environment. According to BB, *"... people always do not like change"*. He felt that people, in general, are resistant to changes proposed to the system. For example, the development team is always looking forward to delivering code to the production environment as fast as possible. On the other hand, operations personnel prefer to push back on changes because they are interested in keeping the production environment stable. It is an illustration of, *"people resisting to this DevOps movement, some people still think there are better off with their waterfall way of doing work" [BB]*. Therefore, such resistance negatively affects the interaction between development and operations teams as it gives rise to feelings that prevent team engagement, involvement, team coordination and trust. Lack of all these essential elements negatively affect the structural and relational dimensions of team social capital.

The participants felt that DevOps teams are expected to work together to ensure continuous integration, deployment, and delivery (CI/CD). Hence, according to AL, *"wherever we've been trying to make improvements, this has been met with resistance, e.g. Agile project management on the Rally tool. Only recently, have we been able to start having an impact on the conversation"*. The issue here is not about the tool but is rather about how the tool enables better collaboration between the teams, makes the progress of work more visible and improve communication between the DevOps teams. The participant felt not everybody realized the need for this because some people were resistant to the idea that implementing Rally will improve team collaboration. It points back to the issue of a lack of team collaboration, which harms the relational dimension of team social capital within the teams.

4.1.2.2 Poor Staff Retention and Job Security

Das and Baruah (2013) described staff retention as the organisation's intent to retain certain employees with specialised knowledge and skills and not lose them to other competing organisations. They found that there is a strong relationship between staff retention and job security. In other words, staff retention promotes job security through the assurance of continued employment. Most of the participants acknowledged that, where there is job security, team members' commitment increases.

JA, a contractor indicated that, *"they sometimes feel threatened by contract re-negotiations ..."*. Contract renewals may not turn out well. While the outcome of the negotiations are not finalized, contracted team members are uncertain of their future. This affects their ability to think and concentrate as well as their participation in the team If the negotiations lead to termination of contracts, it leaves collaboration and knowledge gaps within DevOps teams, which affects both relational and cognitive dimensions of team social capital. According to DJ, *"Everybody is living in fear, worried about their jobs. In the ideal world the organisation can put job security forward as a given therefore team synergy follows"*. Team members' participation is perceived to increase when they know that their job is secured, and they are happy with their contracts. However, some team members are not certain that their job is secured. This gives rise to feelings of insecurity and lack of trust which prevent team participation, engagement and yield low morale. A low team morale prevents the interactions between team members which includes positive communication and sharing work related tasks. Lack of participation in the team also limits knowledge sharing and collaboration. *"Team social capital in this environment is broken, the current environment people are not sure whether their jobs are safe or not. There is a lot of uncertainty and people are fearful of losing their jobs."* *[DJ]*. The participants pointed out that job insecurity negatively affects the structural, relational and cognitive dimensions of team social capital.

JA pointed out that, *"there is a strong divide between contractors and permanent staff, we have had contractors in our team that have been working for us for 16 years and it's still seen as them and us, as they are not seen as part of the family, they are sort of step children"*. He noted that these divisions among DevOps team members harm team collaboration, team cohesion, and shared norms. Furthermore, he started that, *"it's bizarre because we are all working for the same common cause, even though they have got an extra deal working for the contracting house on extra requirement"*. Participants exhibited that the "us versus them" attitude overlooks the essential principles of DevOps, which in turn inhibits the three dimensions of team social capital.

4.1.2.3 Poor Work-Life Balance

According to Kalliath and Brough (2008), work-life balance is the individual perception that work and non-work activities are compatible. Chan et al (2016) noted that work–life balance had a positive impact on job and family satisfaction.

"The biggest issue is I am typically on 24/7 standby for the last 20 years. I have been on standby most of the time. I cannot go away. I must be close to home or work ... so I can address problems. My social life is restricted and when I do go away on leave, I must organise standby. It's always an issue because it's always difficult to find someone with equal technical skills because I do different stuff e.g. Oracle DBA, OS side, Network side and Web server side.SO, it's always difficult to find all standby to assist when you are not there" [BB]. The participant pointed out that because of limited skilled and experienced team members, the work cannot be transferred to underutilized team members so that the workload is shared proportionally and have a rotation on standbys. The participant felt more urgent work gets assigned to experienced team members, and there is no one to assist or relieve them. They end up restricting their social lives. In the end, the workload leads to burnout and work-related stress. Hence, impairing the three dimensions of team social capital.

"In this DevOps environment, the work becomes 24/7, doing development and operations. There has never been a case where, I have done development, and I don't have to worry about it ever again. I will only be phoned in case something goes wrong but now it's like, once I have done the development and I must support as well" [JA]. The participant highlighted that with the nature of work in a DevOps environment, the workload grows to accommodate both development and operations work. Once development is completed team members are expected to be on the support line to address production issues. The participants felt the result is that team members will suffer from work-related pressure and struggle to balance work and personal life. Consequently, the team members' morale, mood, behavior, and performance in the team are negatively affected and lead to diminished team social capital.

4.2 Organisational Factors

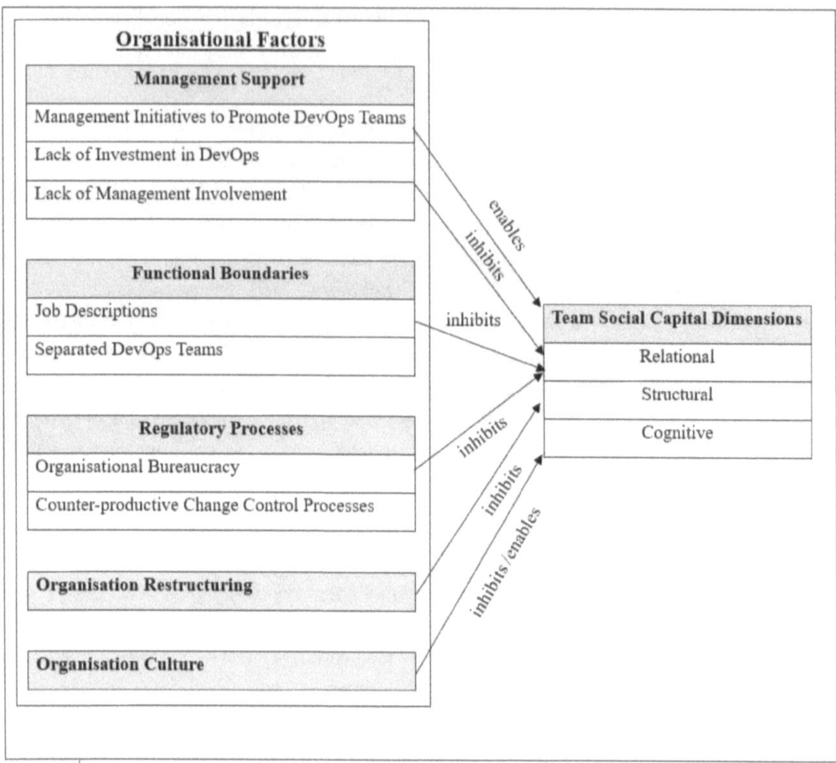

Figure 4.2: Organisational Factors

Greenberg and Baron (1995) defined an organisation as a structured social system consisting of groups and individuals working together to accomplish common objectives. The participants identified the following organizational factors that influence the dimensions of team social capital and therefore team synergy: (1) Management Support, (2) Functional Boundaries, (3) Regulatory Processes, (4) Organisation Restructuring, and (5) Organisation Culture

4.2.1 Management Support

The participants described management support as the willingness of management to get involved and support teams in achieving their DevOps objectives. They identified the following themes relating to management support: 1) Management Initiatives to promote DevOps teams, (2) Lack of investment in DevOps, and (3) Lack of management involvement.

4.2.1.1 Management Initiatives to Promote DevOps Teams

According to MM, *"it is well documented that agile practices such as DevOps needs management support and if that is not present, it is very difficult to get it up and running. The organisation must create an infrastructure for ideas to surface"*. The participant highlighted that management should create a work environment where new ideas are welcome and nurtured. Stressing the same point, LC stated that, *"when there is initiative from management to promote DevOps teams, you find that people's minds change to adapt and apply DevOps practices. If you get the buy-in from there and from a CIO level or whatever management level and they are willing to make the changes on organisational perspectives, then you find that peoples' minds can easily change to adapt to that process and all the underlying blockages, the environment, the knowledge sharing that cross-team function will not take too long to resolve"*. The participants stated that management's initiatives to support DevOps teams show commitment to promoting DevOps practices. Team members can easily change their mindset towards DevOps, knowing that management is behind them, in full support. Consequently, it boosts better team relationships and alleviates team collaboration and knowledge sharing, which promotes the relational and cognitive dimensions of team social capital. Therefore, achieving team synergy between development and IT operations teams.

According to NP, *"More recently there has been a drive to promote DevOps practices to try and leverage all the good things DevOps team seem to have. Nobody stands in a way of that being done. The organisation is supportive of it when it makes technical and financial sense"*.TT also acknowledged that the organisation *"... try to encourage people a lot, so we are all part of the same team and we all part of same goal."*. Again, the participants acknowledged that a drive from management to promote DevOps practices enables DevOps teams to achieve the dimensions of team social capital. The development and operations teams see themselves as one team working together to achieve a common objective.

4.2.1.2 Lack of Investment in DevOps

The focus of DevOps is on building cross-functional teams. Investment in the right skills, infrastructure, and training is needed to create cross-functional teams (Cuppett, 2016; Hussain, Clear, & MacDonell, 2017; Senapathi, Buchan, & Osman, 2018). The participants revealed that a lack of investment in the right tools, resources, and training hinders the teams from achieving their DevOps goals, for instance, collaboration, knowledge sharing and efficiency in coordinating their tasks.

"I feel it's worth has been thrown away. I don't feel the organisation understands its true depth, I don't feel they understand the benefits of DevOps that can be obtained once you get everyone involved and pulling their weight on it and successfully backing it and so that sets the undertone. So, there is word around it but there is no investment" [LC].

"Something basically, they should do is providing the necessary tools, resources and training to the people is very crucial" [MM].

The participants felt that when management invests in the necessary tools, resources, and training, it shows that management understands the benefits of DevOps and the need to get everyone involved. Then, it will improve the quality of service and the expertise of team members in applying DevOps practices. However, the participants exhibited that there is limited investment in the required DevOps tools, resources, and training. Insufficient resources, training, and limited investment of DevOps tools lead to limited collaboration and exchange of information among the DevOps teams. It also makes it difficult for the development and operations team to coordinate their work effectively. As a result, it impairs the three dimensions of team social capital.

4.2.1.3 Lack of Management Involvement

Young and Jordan (2008) defined management involvement as devoting time to a project in proportion to its cost and potential, reviewing plans, following up on results, and facilitating the management problems involved with integrating with the management process of the business. Therefore, management participation plays a significant function in creating the conditions required for team synergy to exist.

"There is a vision of where we want to be with DevOps but because of those constraints, and the funding element and the non-CIO involvement, it creates a situation where the team does not see the benefits of DevOps and the potentials you reach with it" [LC]

"DevOps needs management support and involvement. If that is not present, it is very difficult to get it up and running." [MM]

The participants revealed that lack of management involvement creates conditions in which development and operations teams are unable to reach their DevOps goals and are not realizing the benefits of applying DevOps effectively. Lack of management involvement is an indication that management is not fully committed to supporting DevOps teams to reach their objectives. Team members feel less motivated when management is not involved in driving their team activities. As an outcome, it inhibits the dimensions of team social capital because there is no management drive to ensure the teams are meeting their DevOps objectives, which are team collaboration, sharing of information and tasks.

4.2.2 Functional Boundaries

DevOps practices are in favor of removing functional boundaries to adapt to cross-functional teams (Cagle, Rice, & Kristan, 2015; König, & Steffens, 2018). The aim is to stimulate shared responsibilities between development and operations teams. However, the participants revealed that the existing organization structure still has not eliminated the traditional boundaries between development and operations teams. The participants identified the following in connection with functional boundaries: (1) Job descriptions and (2) Separated DevOps teams.

4.2.2.1 Job Descriptions

A job description defines the roles and responsibilities entitled to a team member's job specification. The participants revealed that while some team members are willing to perform tasks outside their stipulated job description, others are reluctant to go beyond that. Moreover, the participants mentioned that some team members use their stipulated job descriptions as an excuse to resist change, which they believe is a set back to the structural and relational dimensions of team social capital.

"With having defined roles, some people use that against change. Job descriptions, say for instance, a developer would say I am not a system administrator. It has happened with some people in the past. They will not do anything other than what is in their job description or piece of paper. Yet they don't necessarily see it on the end as an opportunity to broaden themselves" [NP]

"People limit themselves in a situation where the individual stays within the bounds of the job description. There is a different situation where the individual does more than what their Job Descriptions (JDs) or their roles and responsibilities outline, and I find that those individuals in that capacity finds it easier to cross between the different roles" [LC]

The participants confirmed that DevOps requires team members with various technical and social skills as well as those who are willing to have a blend of skills that go beyond their job descriptions. However, in the context of this study, some team members preferred to stay in their fixed roles and responsibility and denied themselves the learning opportunities presented through interactions, sharing of responsibilities, and tasks between the development and operations teams. Therefore, strict adherence to fixed roles and responsibilities impede DevOps teams from achieving the structural, relational and cognitive dimensions of team social capital. As a result, it impairs the synergy between development and operations teams.

On the other hand, participants also noted that going beyond the stipulated job description can lead to inappropriate and undermining behaviors. For example, while getting involved in tasks that are beyond their job description, some individuals irritated their fellow team members. *"We tend to cross a lot of boundaries just to get things done, it can be problematic if you are stepping on other people's toes and that can negatively affect the relationships and then they not going to like working with you again"[JA]* Such circumstances lead to poor team relationships and negatively influence team social capital. Furthermore, it harms the DevOps culture where team cohesion, team collaboration, trust, and shared understanding are expected to exist.

4.2.2.2 Separated DevOps Teams

DevOps integrates development and IT operations teams, and at the same time emphases communication and collaboration, continuous integration, quality assurance, and delivery with automated deployment utilizing a set of development practices (Ebert, Gallardo, Hernantes, & Serrano, 2016; Erich, 2018). One of the goals of DevOps is to foster synergy between development and operations personnel, to improve organizational efficiency (Nybom, Smeds, & Porres, 2016). However, the participants revealed that their existing organizational structure consists of separated DevOps teams, which they feel is a hinderance to the dimensions of team social capital and the synergy between development and operations teams.

"In the current structure, and what the organisation aims, they try to promote that collapse of the roles and boundaries, but people are still sort of bound to that, development only want to see what they want to see and what they used to see. Support still say the same thing that the development function should stay in development, that's where you keep it, where DevOps is one view regardless of what your role is" [LC]

"I see it as negative because you have these silos and getting help from another silo is sometimes difficult" [LS]

The participants explained that DevOps teams in which development and operations have clear disparate roles imply a misunderstanding of DevOps as a concept. The development and operations teams exist as separate functions. DevOps is a cultural movement encouraging the integration of development and operations teams into one team to improve communication and collaboration. Therefore, separate development and operations teams potentially generates communication barriers and delayed feedback loops. Communication barriers negatively affect team collaboration, making it difficult for DevOps teams to work together. Team members work in silos, which give rise to a lack of openness and sharing of task-related information and knowledge. The participants exhibited that separating development and operations teams prevent the dimensions of team social capital, and therefore lack lacks support for team synergy.

However, LS further revealed that separating development and operations functions is a security measure, for instance, *"they should be boundaries there because you have things like security issues that your average developer might not be aware of, but your specialist Database Administrator (DBA) might know better than you do"*. The participant felt that the development team might not have the same understanding and awareness of the security risks as the database administrators. Development team members are used to experiment and try out things, and it is difficult for operations team members to trust developers with the production system. The participant further revealed that the split between development and operations is influenced by the Sarbanes-Oxley Act, stating that,*" that development and operations should be separated so that things like back doors cannot be built into production and you cannot have a developer accessing and modifying production data and vice-versa production person building in a back door in the development code for example, for their own nefarious purposes" [LS].* The participant revealed that separation of duties between development and operations teams is done to achieve compliance and also reduce the chances of security breaches. On the other hand, the participant felt that these requirements are disruptive to the changing IT environment where DevOps practices are applied. Instead of breaking the wall of conflict between development and operations teams, separation of duties create a reinforced wall between the DevOps teams. As a result, it impairs the elements of team social capital and the expected synergy required for DevOps teams to function efficiently and effectively.

4.2.3 Regulatory Processes

According to Rance (2011), IT organizations implement regulatory processes to protect the services they deliver to the business. For example, regulatory processes could be put in place to mitigate the risks of introducing unsafe code in the production environment. The participants identified that the following themes are related to regulatory processes: (1) organizational bureaucracy and (2) counter-productive change control processes.

4.2.3.1 Organizational bureaucracy

According to LS, *"... being a large organisation, there are so many processes in place, and it seems we are struggling with red tape a lot. For example, just getting a database user created on your database can sometimes take 3 to 4 days, such a very simple thing to do. It's not like it's difficult, getting access to a system. So, there is a lot red tape around the organisation which breaks your speed, slow you down".* She felt that such a simple request should not take that long to complete, but it is not always the case. Even a simple task is subjected to follow the process, which is characterized by a never-ending series of reviews and checks to complete, resulting in painfully long days before the change can be implemented, at the same time breaking the agility and the spirit of the teams. According to JA, *"it is frustrating being limited to deliver software when you can release because the customers want it urgently but I must go through – document this, create this process, fill in this form, apply for this permission. You will see that something that only takes 2 hours will take something like 3 days before I can deliver the software."* The participants felt that these over-bureaucratic procedures are time-consuming, and it limits the development and operations teams to coordinate their tasks and apply DevOps practices effectively. As a result, it impairs both structural and relational dimensions of team social capital.

4.2.3.2 Counter-productive change control processes

The participants unveiled that the change control processes slow down the speed for continuous integration and delivery. MM stated that, *"the current organisation is set up for governance and for protecting against change. The governance process consists of a Change Control Board. For any changes proposed to the system, must go through the change control board for approval. You must complete a change order and submit to the change control board where it gets an implementation pin and schedule date. This whole process can take sometimes 4 to 6 months to get approval and implement the change into production."* The participant felt that these counter-productive change control processes are still based on traditional methodologies and they do not align well with the cross-functional nature of DevOps. For example, the process of documentation introduces delays on DevOps processes, which the participants considered as counterproductive and unnecessary blockage to team collaboration. As a result, it inhibits the relational dimension of team social capital. *"We in quite a rapid application development type of life cycle, where we can constantly change and deploy anywhere but i must go through - i need to document this, create this process, fill in this form, apply for this permission. You will see that something that only takes 2 hours will take something like 3 days before I can deliver to a customer. It is just very irritating - but - that's life."* [JA] The change control processes are ineffective and counterproductive as they lengthen the DevOps life cycle times and feedback loops, which negatively the dimensions of team social capital. The participants felt that the whole process drives them to the wall as longer feedback loops give rise to misalignment between the teams and slow down the exchange of task-related information and knowledge among the DevOps team members. Further, it negatively affects the communication and interaction between the team members.

4.2.4 Organisation Restructuring

Organizational restructuring involves changing the size and structure of the organisation (Zweni, 2004). The objective of restructuring is to reduce the number of employees through retrenchments, assuming the organization performs effectively. The participants highlighted that the organization went through a restructuring exercise in the form of staff retrenchments, resignations, and Voluntary Severance Packages (VSP) /Voluntary Early Retirement Packages (VERP). They pointed out that it was a drawback to the teams, losing key team members, and in turn, created gaps within the existing teams' social ties.

"Organisation structure changes and movements in and out around the company has an immense impact on an individual's thinking pattern" [LC]

"We have seen the dangers of it, losing skills in the analysis space. The organisation does not have good handover processes, it's a problem in the organisation structure when some is leaving the company" [MS]

"Team synergy can get destroyed because people disappear then hmm ..., I suppose when you focus on what is required it's always a good thing, then people start saying I am no longer in this role or responsibility. I can't help you with that, then you have taken business knowledge and you have written it off" [JA]

Employees that left the organization went away with their skills, knowledge, and experience. The remaining team members are constrained to closing all the gaps left by their ex-team members, resulting in excessive workload. The participants felt that individuals who left the organization did so without proper handovers taking place to ensure knowledge transfer. Therefore, the teams lost knowledge and experience without replenishing it, a drawback to the cognitive dimension of team social capital. The participants acknowledged that the restructuring disrupted existing DevOps teams' social ties, which influenced knowledge sharing, reduced team coordination, and task completion. Therefore, it is a drawback to the cognitive and relational dimensions of team social capital and a breakdown of the synergy between development and operations.

4.2.5 Organisation Culture

Organizational culture describes the way of doing things within the organization, which includes undocumented rules that influence individual and team behavior and attitudes (Parker, & Bradley, 2000; Sun, 2008). The DevOps paradigm instills a change in organisational culture to promote collaboration, automation, sharing, continuous integration, and delivery software. (Rajkumar, Pole, Adige, & Mahanta, 2016; Forsgren, & Humble, 2016; Wiedemann, 2018). The participants revealed that applying DevOps practices is a cultural shift aimed to promote team synergy between the development and operations teams. Therefore, for this cultural shift to happen smoothly, the behavior and attitudes of the employees, values, and traditions, and management and leadership styles should be aligned.

"The organisation should set the tone and create an atmosphere that allows a mindset shift to happen harmoniously" [MM]. "If ... CIO ... management ... they are willing to make the changes on organisational perspectives, then you find that peoples' minds can easily change to adapt to that process" [LC]. The participants assert that an organization culture can either support or neglect change. Changing the way people work involves a change in culture and this change should be driven by the organization's culture. LC stated that, *"cultural change is driven by the organisation and will feed it all the way down to all its employees. It's a mindset change and with that as I mentioned about the roles and where conflict occurs between development and operations teams, this is what DevOps resolves. Within the organisation, people's mindset need to change in order to understand that DevOps is a cultural shift and in order take that and apply it"* The participants felt that a DevOps culture which is set and driven by the organization creates a conducive environment to ensure there are no silos between development and operations teams. The organization supports a culture of shared

responsibilities, which encourages closer collaboration and trust among the DevOps teams. By doing so, it promotes the structural, relational and cognitive dimensions of team social capital.

"The wall between Dev and Ops partially exist and there are still differences in perspectives and culture. The culture is also another thing, but the culture can change if you have the conducive environment to change." [BB] Combining development and operations functions can be relatively simple and straightforward. However, the concept may turn out to be difficult when cultural differences still exist between development and operations teams. The organization should create a conducive environment by creating a common culture and drive that from top management to the operational level. Cultural differences increase the chances of team conflicts to occur, which breaks the trust and collaborations as well as negatively impacting how DevOps teams coordinate their work. Hence, inhibiting the three dimensions of team social capital. According to LC, *"all the underlying blockages, the environment, the knowledge sharing that cross-team function will take too long to resolve because cultural differences. If that does not change, it's extremely difficult. So, that's a cultural and a mind shift change, more at the top"*

4.3 Task Characteristics

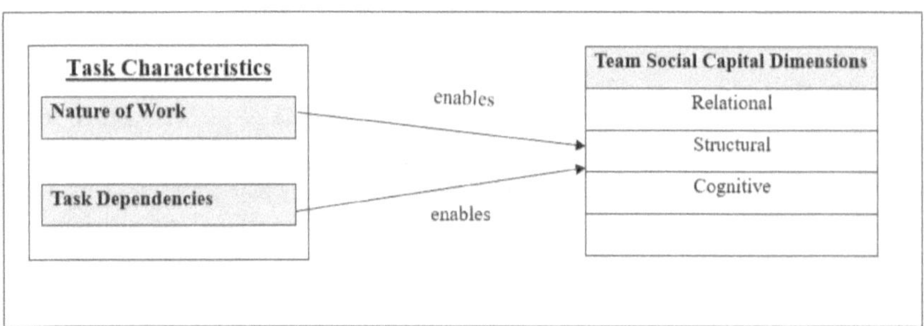

Figure 4.3: Task Characteristics

In this section, the participants described the nature and structure of their work and how it contributes to the dimensions of team social capital. Furthermore, the participants discussed how good management of task dependencies between the teams to promote dimensions of team social capital.

4.3.1 Nature of Work

The nature of the work described by the participants reflects the activities carried out throughout the DevOps life cycle. Bass, Weber, and Zhu (2015) revealed the phases of the DevOps life cycle as requirements, development, build, testing, deployment, and execution.

The participants revealed that the nature of their DevOps work involves dealing with multiple projects simultaneously, and the work is organised in such a way that complex projects are prioritized. LC stated, *"We work in process where there are multiple projects and Change Requests (CRs) running in parallel of each other. How our work is organised in DevOps teams currently is that we focus on the most complex projects and that allows us to work together with the product owner, so we sort of follow that process where the product owner is involved from the beginning"* The participant felt that dealing with multiple projects at the same time encourages DevOps teams to organise and prioritise their work, which allow them to identify which projects and tasks should be dealt with first. Also, the participant revealed that having to handle a complex project entices the team members to collaborate and engage with other stakeholders such as the product owner. Team collaboration further promotes the relational dimension of team social capital.

Also, TT mentioned that, *"most of the time we work in SharePoint and SharePoint itself is a collaboration tool. We try by all means to ensure that all work-related documentation is booked in SharePoint, central and same location for everyone to be able to contribute."* The participant revealed that most of their work, which consists of both development and operations activities, is visible for everyone in SharePoint, a collaboration tool that allows DevOps teams to share their task-related information. Therefore, both relational and cognitive dimensions of team social capital are achieved through team collaboration and knowledge sharing, through the use of a collaborative software.

4.3.2 Good Management of Task Dependencies

Task dependencies occur when a task cannot progress before another task is completed. The progress of the task is blocked or delayed. According to MM, *"task dependencies takes very different shapes or forms but during the initial phases we do identify dependencies. There are social and technical ways of dealing with task dependencies. It is very essential that when you have these task dependencies exist, teams involved should work together to manage those dependencies and not let the dependencies impede the team's progress."* The participants identified the following practices relating to managing task dependencies: daily standup meetings, use of backlogs, and project planning.

During daily standup meetings, team members inform each other of their work activities and highlight existing impediments. According to JA, *"We normally have daily meetings on what is required. We assist where we can if things really don't go according to plan"*. In the same context, LC explained, *"If there's dependencies identified within a task, it's a question of, before committing and once we do the estimation and that point of time have a discussion with the product owner. We try to get to a point where the constraints or issues are identified and addressed before committing to a sprint"*. The participants felt that daily stand-ups enable team members to manage dependencies by discussing roles and responsibilities and engage with different stakeholders. It shows that the teams work together to identify the best solutions to address any mitigating circumstances. Therefore, the participants highlighted managing task dependencies through daily standup meeting promotes the existence of team social capital dimensions, which lead to team synergy.

The teams' participation and continuous engagement are required to manage task dependencies using backlogs. The participants indicated that if there are task dependencies identified, the teams involved discuss with the product owner before removing the task from the current sprint. According to LC, *"It is a point of going back and unpacking it and getting that essence whether that task can be pushed back into the product backlog or to be addressed in a different sprint if it's a showstopper."* The participants felt that managing dependencies through backlogs promote team members and all stakeholders to work together to identify what should go in and out of the backlog. LS mentioned that, *"project planning especially with the high complexity on the project we are working on, they brought in a dedicated project planner, to plan our tasks, with that it comes with dependencies, so we determine the dependencies so that we can plan the resources and project"*. When DevOps teams are involved in backlog planning to account for existing task dependencies it promotes continuous team engagement and collaboration among them. Therefore, promoting team social capital dimensions which lead to team synergy.

4.4 Team Characteristics

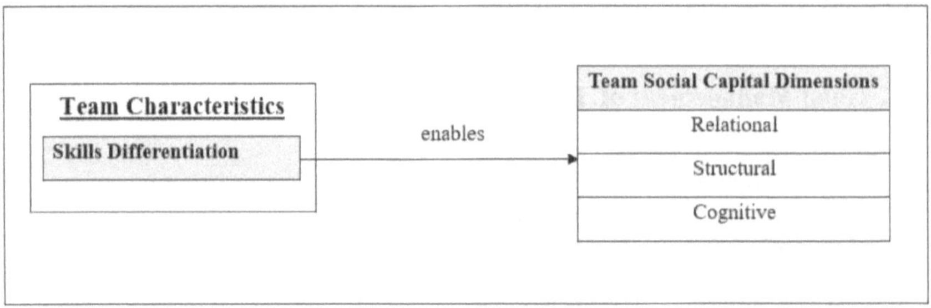

Figure 4.4: Team Characteristics

Lee, Koopman, Hollenbeck, Wang, and Lanaj (2015) described skills differentiation as the degree to which teams consist of members with specialized and diverse knowledge or skills that make them uniquely qualified for their roles. In DevOps teams, skill differentiation enable team members to rely on each other's unique knowledge and skill sets to perform well and achieve their common goals (Wiedemann, Wiesche, & Kremar, 2018). The participants revealed that skills differentiation within the DevOps teams can positively impact the dimensions of team social capital.

"We have different skill levels within the team i.e. junior and senior team members, I have strong skills in software delivery, and I play a team lead role for some of the projects" [TT]. DevOps requires team members with diverse skills i.e. process skills, automation skills, functional skills, technical and soft skills. *"Some of our team members have strong and specialised skills in Oracle which is always good if you are stuck trying to get something done then if they are very approachable speak to them, they will help you out. Other guys have got important skills on the network and infrastructure side. If you have a problem you can approach them. It's quite important to have like a wide variety of skillsets that team members can all contribute" [JA].* The participants highlighted that the teams consist of a diversity of specialized skills covering different areas of the DevOps life cycle. A diversity of skills broaden individual team members skills and knowledge through collaboration, since the skills are spread throughout the DevOps team members. The participants mentioned that this diversity of skills bring development and operations teams together. In the process they collaborate, exchange knowledge and coordinate their task activities effectively. Furthermore, skill differentiation promotes close relationships between team members' trust and team performance. The presence of team collaboration, trust, knowledge sharing and team coordination promote the three dimensions of team social capital.

4.5 Individual Team Members' Characteristics

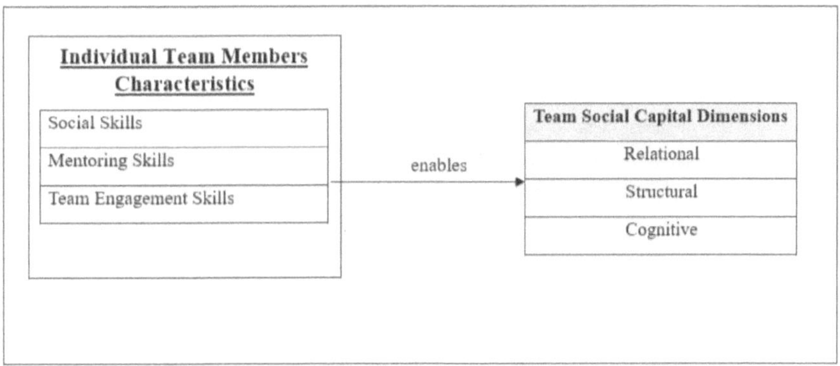

Figure 4.5: Individual Team Members Characteristics

This section discusses how the individual team members' characteristics influence dimensions of team social capital. In particular, an individual's knowledge, skills, and abilities and their influence on the dimensions of team social capital will be described.

According to Chung and Bang (2016), knowledge, skills and abilities should support the pillars of DevOps namely collaboration, automation, measurement of processes and technical metrics, and the sharing of knowledge. In this study, the participants identified the following knowledge, skills and abilities (KSA) as enablers of team social capital: social skills, mentoring skills and engagement skills.

4.5.1 Social Skills

According to LS, *"We all have technical skills because we are already doing our jobs i.e. being able to program in a specific language ... more important are the soft skills ... i.e. ability to search for answers and apply the information"*. The participant pointed out that technical skills are required for team members to accomplish their work activities but soft skills also known as social skills are more important. These skills include the ability and willingness to share, communicate and interact with other team members. Thereby, the teams can collaborate and develop good working relationships. Positive communication and effective task sharing also facilitate team cohesion, which reflects positive interactions between development and operations team members. Hence, enabling the structural dimension of team social capital. Also, the interactions between DevOps team members and their willingness to share task-related information and knowledge promotes relational and cognitive dimension of team social capital.

NP stated that, *"from a more social aspect, I promote team activities like team lunches, we try to have that every three months not only when people are leaving the organisation. And, to mix the team up a bit with regards to who usually works with each other, they try to mix that up to get different people to work with other people in the team."* These team activities encourage team members to socialize outside work and discuss their work and personal experiences. In so doing, it encourages team members to build team relationships, which lead to the development of a common language, shared perspectives, shared narratives, and shared codes. These are also key elements that enable team social capital, and the formation of team synergy.

4.5.2 Mentoring skills

The second KSA that was revealed in the data is mentoring skills. According to MM, *"I coach them into working shorter cycles and getting them to communicate with each other and trying to resolve impediments they might have in their work. I give them advice and ideas on how to solve specific issues they are dealing. I do a lot of physical work setting up deployment pipelines sorting out the code organising how unit testing can be done and can be deployed easily and a lot work keeping the backlog clean and well organised".* On the same note, LS shared that she, *"really enjoy guiding, generally when I deliver something, it's working and it's not usual for it to have errors, so a degree of accuracy there".* Not all the DevOps team members have in-depth knowledge of the DevOps life cycle and how to address issues in a DevOps environment when they arise. The participants found mentoring skills helpful to those team members as they learn and upskill themselves through guidance from the experienced team members. As a result, it promotes skills and knowledge sharing, cross-functional team relationships, and trust, which allow DevOps team members to build the skills needed to carry out their DevOps tasks effectively. Furthermore, skills and knowledge transfer through mentorship promote cognitive and relational dimensions of team social capital.

4.5.3 Team Engagement skills

The third KSA that emerged from the data is team engagement. According to LC, *"understanding things from a development perspective, the project management aspect of it, allows me to be fully involved with stakeholders and business owners and involvement with product owners. I also have a little bit of background on the support perspective and understanding of the infrastructure component that ties with application architecture"* She revealed that team engagement skills reflects team members' commitment towards achieving their DevOps goals. For example, *"creating team synergy is about bridging the gap between development and support personnel from a point of understanding norms. If there is a level of understanding shared amongst the two and that everyone is fully on board and committed to that will greatly alleviate you going forward when working on a project and then fully visibility where projects concerns. If there are changes that occurs on the Dev side itself, recognising and making them available also to the support personnel, so we use Azure DevOps pipeline as a means to communicate if there is coevolution to be done. The full pipeline is visible to all the stakeholders."*

According to MS, *"it is important to identify the people you need to involve. Interact with users and technical people and to create meaningful functional and technical specifications. Identify from a technical perspective the impact of implementing new requirements. skills to gather and understand the requirements".* He added that, *"I believe my contribution is aligning myself with the people I interact with I can build my work more efficiently".* AL also reported that *"in our environment, the role of an analyst is that of the 'glue' between various teams, people and systems".* Furthermore, LC stated that, *"team engagement assist in making the team synergy succeed, to get the deliverables out and sort out the blockages as soon as possible. So, having that knowledge shared amongst the role players it allows a proactive engagement to want to succeed."* She continued, *"We deal with complex projects, anything in excess of 3 to 6 months and there is obviously engagement with the product owner, the structuring of the product backlog items, the estimation element associated with it and the estimation on requirements.*

We document it in Azure DevOps. All the role players including development and operations teams are fully involved in these processes." The participants indicated that team engagement skills assist DevOps teams to achieve team synergy. With team engagement skills, DevOps team members are able to interact and deal with complex projects. In the process, they build trust for each other through sharing information and knowledge to solve complex issues and blockages they encounter. Hence, enabling the three dimensions of team social capital. Also, to note, team engagement is one of the components that promote the relational dimension of team social capital.

4.6 Team Processes

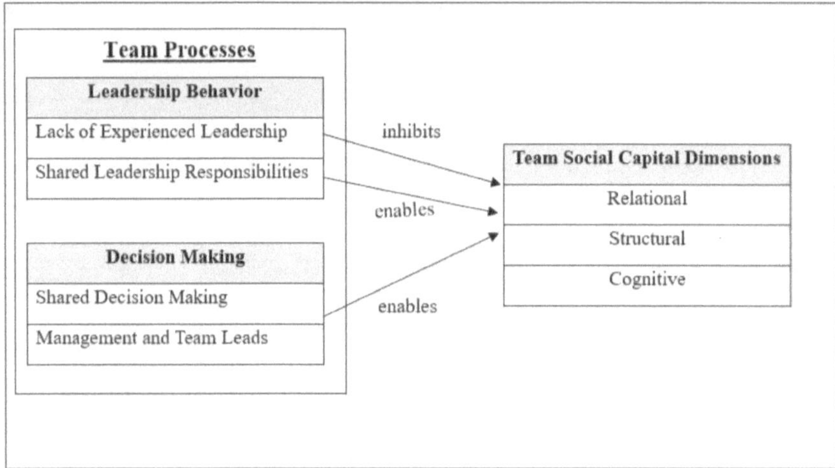

Figure 4.6: Team Processes

According to Costa, Passos, and Bakker (2014), team members engage in interactive actions that transform inputs to outcomes through cognitive, verbal, and behavioral activities directed towards organizing task activities to achieve collective goals. Team processes require DevOps team members to interact each other including operating environment. Processes are also used to direct, align, and monitor what team members are doing. In this section, the participants described following team processes that contribute to the dimensions of team social capital: (1) Leadership behavior and (2) Decision making.

4.6.1 Leadership Behavior

According to Jordan (2016), leadership behavior describes a set of actions, taken by individuals to motivate and encourage others through empowerment processes, engagement, and collaborative assignments to meaningful work. Since Ravichandran, Taylor, and Waterhouse (2016) asserted that DevOps practice entails building new shared values and behaviors across development and operations teams, good leadership behavior could play an active role in promoting these values. Relating to leadership behavior, the following themes were identified as inhibitors and enablers of the dimensions of team social capital: (1) Lack of experienced leadership and (2) Shared leadership responsibilities.

- **Lack of Experienced Leadership**

Some of the participants felt that management does not have the right leadership skills to drive a DevOps culture across the teams. They highlighted that a lack of experienced leadership is an inhibitor to the dimensions of team social capital, preventing development and operations teams from achieving the desired synergy.

NA stated that, *"our technical leadership is very weak, at the moment extremely weak. From a technically strategic decision-making point of view, causing the DevOps environment to be extremely unstable."* She further explained that, *"the environment is unstable because of all the organisational changes (restructuring exercise), loss of knowledgeable resources, the mood is low, there is no clear leadership, there is no steadfast clear leadership"* The participant pointed out that the lack of experienced leadership negatively affects the team members' morale and it creates instability in the DevOps environment. Low team morale leads to insecurity, which limits their involvement and engagement. As a result, it inhibits structural and relational dimensions of team social capital.

On the other hand, LS stated that, *"at this stage we are sitting with a leader who doesn't have the experience and obviously it's not going as smooth as it could but on the flip side of the coin, we have all been together for too long and we know what we need to do. We are not in such strong need of that leadership because of the experience that we have in our team"* She argued that with the experience the team members have, the teams can manage and organise themselves without the need for strong and experienced leadership. Also, MM stated that, *"the leadership thing is obviously an old thing. In Agile and DevOps, you do not have the old leadership style of manager and subordinates. The leadership is divided among members with very clear roles and responsibilities."* Some of the participants argued that there is no for a strong leader since DevOps leadership is shared among team members. The preferred leadership style in a DevOps environment is where team members organise themselves and share leadership responsibilities.

- **Shared Leadership Responsibilities**

In a DevOps environment, autonomous teams work collaboratively across the development and operations departments and share leadership responsibilities. Some of the participants revealed that when both development and operations participate and share technical leadership responsibilities, ownership is shared which contributes to the DevOps teams' overall success. This promotes team social capital, which leads to the achievement of team synergy.

"We have a manager who is multi-functional. The leadership is understood but the standards are always shifting. It can be good or bad for us sometimes" [MS].

"The technical leadership that I am exposed to is quite hands-on and of high quality. The manager is very pedantic (in a good sense) about software quality and good designs, formal design reviews are enforced" [AL].

The participants felt that in a situation where the technical leader is involved, it promotes close team relationships and allows development and operations to seek the best options and ideals through collaboration and communication. As a result, it promotes structural dimension of team social capital.

According to BB, the leadership in the team may be *"depending on what area of team you are talking about because each one of us are subject matter experts (SMEs) on different environments"*. The DevOps team may consist of experts in different areas that is automation, CI/CD pipelines, build and release management, security, etc. SMEs are cross-functional experts who facilitate collaboration and ensures the quality, reliability, and stability of all production systems and services while applying DevOps best practices. *"In Agile and DevOps, you do not have the old leadership style of manager and subordinates. The leadership is divided among members with very clear roles and responsibilities" [MM].* SMEs from development and operations work together throughout the phases of the DevOps lifecycle. Everyone in the team feel is responsible for the success of the project. Therefore, shared leadership creates an environment that enables all the dimensions of team social capital, leading to the desired team synergy.

4.6.2 Decision-Making

In DevOps teams, there should be a high degree of autonomy regarding decision making. (Horlach, Drews, Schirmer, & Böhmann, 2017; Wiedemann, 2018; Chen, 2018). Team members have the freedom to discuss matters arising and make collective decisions. In the context of this study, the participants revealed that the decision-making process is shared among the DevOps team members and in some circumstances management and technical leaders are responsible for making decisions on behalf of the teams which both promote the dimensions of team social capital.

- **Shared Decision making**

The participants felt that decisions are shared between teams through a well-managed approach that reduce communication overheads. MM stated that *"the roles are well defined; every group knows exactly which decisions for the team are there to make."* This reveals that the DevOps team members are responsible for making decisions relating to the planning, operations, development, tests, and monitoring. The decision-making responsibilities are completely shared among development and operations team members. Accordingly, TT mentioned that, *"the team members are responsible in making decisions for the work in terms of timelines"*. *"Most of it is given to the team because to try to facilitate just the process. They need to decide among themselves. They must reach an agreement and that whatever the outcome is of that fits into the team norm" [LC].* Team norms are set by the team members to create a shared understanding and promote autonomous decision making. According to the participants, the DevOps team members have the freedom to make collective decisions that influence their services and processes. Team members communicate and interact with each other to make such collective decisions that best suit the norms of the DevOps teams. Hence, promoting the relational and cognitive dimension of social capital.

- **Management and Team Leads**

The participants indicated that management and team leads are also responsible in making decisions. As presented in Figure 4.6, the participant pointed out that a decision-making process where management and team leads are involved promote the dimensions of team social capital.

According to BB, *"the Subject Matter Expert in the domain will be responsible for proposing what decisions to be made and the decision will be made by matter of fact. If the decision influence external teams then it needs to be approved by management"*. Furthermore, JA, a Systems Specialist and Team Lead stated that, *"There is a couple of us that are quite happy to make decisions and we are trusted to make decisions on how things should go. We do collaborate, and we do debate what should be done, and we all manage to come to the same page"*. In a DevOps environment, Subject Matter Experts are primarily responsible in facilitating team collaboration and always seeking opportunities for improving the quality of software delivery. Furthermore, being cross-functional experts, in making decisions they engage with the development and operations teams. Also, working closely with the management, creates an environment where DevOps practices are well-supported. As a result, it builds trust among the DevOps team members knowing that the decision-making is in support of their DevOps initiatives.

In the same context, NP also explained that, *"Decision-making from a technical point of view, is left very much to the team members, with more knowledge, and the junior people would then take the cue from the senior people, with regards to decision making that affects other systems or product releases that where I would say you need to do this"*. The team leads and managers' participation is to ensure that teams decision support a broader DevOps vision across teams and the entire organization. Similar to SMEs, team leads are members in the who have knowledge of the DevOps environment. Therefore, having management and team leaders taking part in making decisions build closer team relationships and trust between the development and operations teams. Also, in the process of making decisions, task-related information and knowledge are exchanged, and team members have the freedom to interact with their team leads. Such interaction and communication between management and the team leaders are essential for DevOps teams because it strengthens feedback loops and better informs decision-making at all management levels. As a result, it promote the structural, relational and cognitive dimensions of team social capital.

4.7 Use of Technology

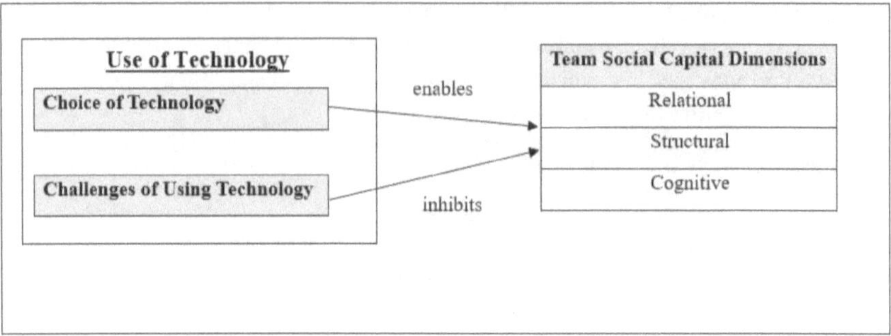

Figure 4.7: Use of Technology

DevOps teams use different technology stacks to facilitate continuous integration, continuous deployment, and delivery of new code into production. The use of these tools strengthens the DevOps mindset of collaboration, integration, and communication (Michelsen, 2013). Participants in this study were able to share some of the technologies used in their DevOps environment and how the use of these technologies affect the dimensions of team social capital. The themes identified relating to the use of technology are as follows: (1) Choice of Technologies and (2) Challenges of using technology.

4.7.1 Choice of Technology

The participants highlighted different technology stacks used within their teams. Their choice of technologies was associated with the chosen DevOps processes and the extent to which the technology supports the desired DevOps functions. Some of the desired objectives for choosing specific technologies mentioned by the participants were communication, collaborative change management, collaborative software development, code repository, and build automation, bug tracking, and modeling and design.

According to TT *"these technologies allow us to communicate in real time which enables us to get instant feedback"*. An important element of the communication process is ensuring that feedback is always reaching the right team members. JA stated that, *"to make DevOps teams work together effectively, it requires the teams to remove obstacles such as communication barriers". We use Skype for business, WebEx and WhatsApp to collaborate. These technologies allow us to communicate in real time which enables us to get instant feedback. [TT]* Fundamentally, the agility of DevOps teams is dependent on team communication. The DevOps methodology is built on creating a loop of continuous feedback and response. Without good communication tools, it becomes difficult for DevOps teams to work together and deliver value to the end users. The participants presented collaborative tools such as WebEx, Skype, WhatsApp, Azure DevOps, Slack, Trello, etc. which indicates that development and operations teams have a common understanding of the tools. It also presents that there is a higher degree of teamwork and shared understanding among the team members when choosing these tools, which positively contribute to the relational and cognitive dimensions of team social capital.

For collaboration, some of the participants revealed that they use tools like Slack and Trello, which enable development and operations teams to work together and their work is made visible through work boards. DevOps team members are able to track and monitor their work in a single dashboard view. Other tools like Team Foundation Server (TFS) and Azure DevOps were also mentioned. According to LC, *"... we are using TFS on premise that more for Kanban, the work board basically, further to that, we are using the Azure DevOps stream that has version control and tracking, on a collaboration level"*. Again, collaboration tools should provide *"one central view for all the stakeholders" [LC]. "Use Microsoft TFS for DevOps. In TFS there is a whole set of features that support collaboration such as tagging individual team members and the information stays centralised" [MM]*. The participants appreciated that these tools ensure that team members have a shared understanding and are effectively coordinating their work together. They shared the same understanding that in a DevOps environment, team collaboration is one of DevOps' underlying principles. Team coordination and collaboration are essential components required to promote the structural and relational dimensions of team social capital. Also, the tools facilitate the exchange and sharing of task-related information which promote the cognitive dimension of team social capital.

4.7.2 Challenges of Using Technology

Although technology enables people to work better and faster, some of the participants revealed that there are challenges encountered when using technology. The challenges include lack of collaboration features in some of the tools and limited knowledge and understanding of the technology, of which the participants felt that they inhibitors to the dimensions of team social capital.

Some of the technologies were reported to have limited collaborative features, hence restricting team members involved in tasks that require work coordination. According to MS, *"some tools like Enterprise Architecture (EA) have limited collaborative features. It's pretty much a personal tool developers or analysts use to make visuals available for everyone to understand"*. He felt that DevOps tools and technologies should help teams to work together more efficiently. If collaboration is a missing feature, it implies that development and operations activities are not easily shared. MM reported that, *"the tools in my opinion is a big lack since there is no drive for it. It is more of cowboy tendencies doing what suits and works for an individual."* MM felt that, instead of encouraging team collaboration, some of the tools promote individual team members to work in isolation.

Some of the participants perceived that some of the challenges experienced while using DevOps technologies are due to team members' limited knowledge of these tools. As highlighted by MM, *"team members are sent on a 4-day training session which is completely insufficient. So, it very difficult to starting up a DevOps environment because people are not on same page due to lack of knowledge on the subjects. One of its biggest downfalls is that the CD (Continuous Delivery) setup of our internal tooling is so complicated which means we are also missing the CD side of things."* The participants felt that due to the lack of knowledge and proper training, team members' participation and contribution is limited. Due to little understanding of the technologies, team members end up rejecting or abandoning the tools. MM stated that, *"we cannot use the tools we want to use because of organisational constraints. The organisation's network is very slow, and it is frustrating"*. His frustration shows team members morale is affected, which in turn affect team relationships and the dimensions of team social capital.

4.8 Knowledge Sharing

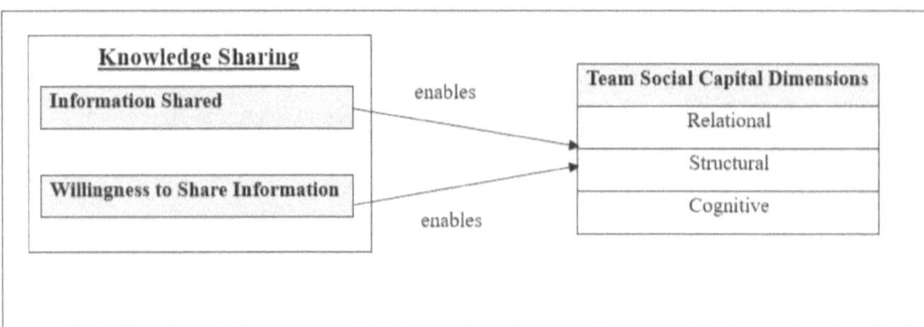

Figure 4.8: Knowledge Sharing

This section describes the participants' experiences and views on how knowledge sharing between development and operations teams influence dimensions of team social capital and team synergy. The section also, presents what kind of information is shared and how it affects the interactions between DevOps team members. Based on the above, the following themes emerged from data (1) Information shared, and (2) Willingness to share information.

4.8.1 Information Shared

DevOps promotes the sharing of information between the development and operations personnel during their release cycles. According to the participants, the information shared mostly consists of code artifacts, release notes, deployment, change configurations, and log files. Sharing information across teams ensures continuous integration of software and efficient DevOps release cycles. The participants asserted that sharing information promotes team members' morale and transparency, encouraging development and operations teams to create trust and mutual respect.

According to LC, she discussed information from two perspectives: *"most of the information shared is from an operational perspective, either it is code base or deployment related. The other one is just following ups as in log files, in the event they want to troubleshoot issues, there is information that surrounds that, predominantly your log files"*. By sharing log files, it prompts DevOps teams to have collective problem solving and troubleshooting. It helps the development and operations teams to fully understand the context of the logged events when logs are shared, enabling them to reach a shared understanding of the problem. The participants perceived that this result in a well-coordinated and collaborated root cause analysis. This joint effort provides team members with an opportunity to participate, share their experiences and perspectives. By so doing, trust and mutual respect continue to build among the teams, which are essential elements of team social capital. Trusting the source of information creates an immeasurable reputation for team collaboration among team members. Therefore, *"... the more information is shared, the more beneficial the relationship between the two teams, Dev and Ops are, because one part knows what the other part is doing in terms of development, configuration and security"* [BB].

Besides log files and deployment-related information, the participants revealed that system documentation such as manuals, guides, specifications, etc. are also shared across the teams. According to LS, *"each of our systems have these guides which tells you exactly what to do, for example if a file system goes faulty, what are you allowed to delete of a file system"*. In the event that processes go down, to restore the process, there is always systems guides to refer to. According to LS, *"That's how it helps the synergy on the team, especially, if the owner of system is not around then the alternate or one of the other guys on the team can refer to the document"*. In the same way, RH revealed that there are, *"guides on how to deploy, support, maintain and monitor. Most of the information is shared on the network so development can see what operations are doing and vice-versa. The guides are open to everybody"*. The participants felt that shared system guides enable team members to have the same understanding of the system and be able to relate events. A shared understanding develops trust among the team members and encourages everybody in the team to contribute positively towards the promotion of team social capital.

The participants believed that with all the information shared, there are some skills transfers taking place between development and operations teams. *"From operations we are very fortunate that we have an understand of development because of our development backgrounds. So, we understand the whole flow from Development to Operations. There is skills transfer between that happens between Development and operations team members, so I am part of the process" [RH].* In a DevOps environment, team members are expected to have an all-rounded process and people skills. RH felt that the information shared facilitate skills transfer and enables team members to expand their DevOps process (lifecycle, automation, integration, deployments, monitoring) and people (interpersonal) skills. For a DevOps team to be successful, it requires team members with the process and people skills. The participants revealed that shared information through knowledge transfer sessions provides DevOps teams the opportunity to develop a sense of trust. When trust exists among the team members, it opens up the other dimensions of team social capital.

4.8.2 Willingness to Share Information

The ability and willingness to share knowledge form the essential soft skills required in a DevOps team. Willingness to share knowledge and information is essential for building a working relationship (Przybilla et al. 2018; Wagner et al. 2014) in DevOps teams. The willingness to share knowledge and experiences overcome obstacles related to common language and culture of team collaboration, enabling DevOps teams to deliver software and infrastructure better and quicker (Cuppett, 2016). The participants revealed that willingness to share information and knowledge leads to a higher degree of communication and collaboration between the development and operations teams. As a result, it boosts the needed cognitive dimension of team social, which contribute to team synergy.

According to JA, *"it is quite important to ensure that everybody in the team is sharing openly so that we can all get an understanding and all work together."* The participant reveals that when DevOps team members share information openly, a common understanding about the task or activity is build, which also encourages the DevOps team members to collaborate. As a result, it promotes relational and cognitive dimensions of team social capital. *"It is extremely important to share knowledge especially technical knowledge. If you discover something that you didn't know you could do, why can't you share with the entire team and we often do it."* *[LS].* The willingness to share task-related information and knowledge within the DevOps team members provide an opportunity for team members to learn from one another enhances their knowledge and effective coordination of team activities. Subsequently, team coordination and the knowledge sharing aspect enables structural and cognitive dimensions of team social capital.

4.9 Summary

In this chapter, the findings of the study were presented. These findings are based primarily on analysis of interviews transcripts and are supported by review documents and observations during the course of the study. Findings were presented based on the theoretical framework. The themes and categories that emerged from the data were aligned to the factors outlined in the theoretical framework. The results of the analysis highlight factors that influence the synergy between development and operations teams in a DevOps environment. Both enabling and inhibiting factors were presented based on the constraints noted in the theoretical framework. The next chapter presents the theoretical explanation of the findings.

Chapter 5: Discussion

The purpose of this study was to identify the factors that influence the synergy between development and IT operations within a DevOps environment. The research was conducted through semi-structured face-to-face interviews with participants from both development and operations backgrounds, and through the review of documents submitted to the researcher. This chapter discusses the findings, in light of the relevant literature, and answers the research questions. The findings are compared to existing literature in order to highlight any new contributions and integrate the concepts with what is already known about the phenomenon under investigation.

The primary objective of the study was to identify the factors that promote or prevent the synergy between development and IT operation teams within a DevOps environment. These factors are discussed based the concepts derived from the theoretical framework presented in Chapter 2. Section 5.1 discusses the factors that promote team synergy between development and IT operations, while section 5.2 discusses the factors that inhibit team synergy between the two teams. Finally, section 5.3 presents a summary of the discussion.

5.1 Factors That Promote Team Synergy

5.1.1 Management Initiatives to Promote DevOps Teams

The study revealed that management initiatives to support DevOps teams plays a crucial role in promoting team synergy. An initiative from management to support DevOps teams enables good team relationships, improves team collaboration, and knowledge sharing, which promote the dimensions of team social capital. This leads to better team synergy between development and IT operations teams. Previous studies that indicate that management's drive to promote DevOps teams encourages team members to network, allowing them to share their experiences and knowledge (Hu & Randel, 2014; Colomo-Palacios, Fernandes, Soto-Acosta, and Larrucea, 2018). This study sheds more light on the role of management by revealing team members embrace the DevOps culture faster when management drives the processes and show full support for DevOps teams.

This study concluded that management initiatives to support DevOps teams demonstrate a commitment to creating an environment that promotes team synergy among DevOps team members. This is in line with past literature on cross-team collaboration (Claps, Svensson, & Aurum, 2015) which found that management commitment is one of the fundamental elements for creating a conducive environment for creating better team relationships, team collaboration, and knowledge sharing (Bucero & Englund, 2015). However, the findings further emphasized how better team relationships, team collaboration, and knowledge sharing contribute positively to the dimensions of team social capital, which result in the synergy between development and IT operations.

Past literature emphasized the importance of management's drive to support DevOps teams in resolving the challenges to DevOps adoption (Riungu-Kalliosaari et al.,2016; Hamunen, 2016; Kamuto & Langerman, 2017). While the previous studies dealt with the challenges in different ways, this study revealed that management's drive to support DevOps teams ensure successful adoption of DevOps practices. This is achieved by promoting the dimensions team social capital, which leads to team synergy between the development and IT operations. Therefore, the results of this study indicate that management initiatives to support DevOps teams promote team synergy between development and operations teams in a DevOps environment.

5.1.2 Good Management of Task Dependencies

According to the findings, good management practices to manage task dependencies such as daily stand-up meetings, use of backlogs and project planning, promote synergy between development and IT operations teams. Stray, Moe, and Aasheim (2019) explained that these practices bring awareness, and knowing who is doing what in the teams is useful information when managing task dependencies. Strode (2016) investigated dependencies in software development projects and found that coordination mechanisms are essential to managing task dependencies. Furthermore, Stray, Moe, and Hoda (2018) maintained that this leads to constant alignment and coordination within DevOps teams. The findings of this study are in line with the literature and confirm that good task management practices play a significant role in promoting team synergy between the development and operations teams.

However, the difference in the outcome of this study compared with previous studies is the emphasis on sound practices to manage task dependencies. The findings further revealed that, in addition to promoting coordination and collaboration, good management of task dependencies play a crucial role in enabling the dimensions of team social capital, through team coordination, knowledge sharing, trust and collaboration among the development and operation teams. Hence, the results of this study indicate that good management practices to manage task dependencies promote team synergy between development and operations teams in a DevOps environment.

5.1.3 Nature of Task

The findings revealed that the nature of work, which consists of both development and IT operations activities, promotes the synergy between development and operations teams when it requires both teams to share and exchange task-related information and knowledge. Furthermore, the study revealed that dealing with multiple and complex projects simultaneously encourages DevOps team members to work together to address challenges emerging from different domains and contexts of work. Therefore, the nature of work presents an opportunity for team members to interact, collaborate, and exchange information, which facilitates the dimensions of team social capital, leading to team synergy. Wiedemann and Wiesche (2018) explained that the nature of work in a DevOps environment requires the development and operations teams to work together, which encourages team collaboration and shared values, understanding as social cohesions. The outcome of this study sheds more light on the type of work that promotes team synergy between development and IT operations teams. For example, the development and operations team work together and share insights on development and infrastructure requirements throughout the DevOps life cycle. This study found that the type work in a DevOps environment, for example, development, deployments and support encourage team coordination, effective communication and continuous feedback between the development and operations teams.

5.1.4 Skill Differentiation

Skill differentiation describes the degree to which members have specialized knowledge or skills that make them uniquely qualified and therefore more or less challenging to substitute (Hollenbeck et al., 2012; Lee et al., 2015). The literature emphasizes that in skill-differentiated teams, team members depend on each other's unique knowledge and skills that are needed for the teams to perform well (De Jong et al.,2016). This study's conclusion that skill differentiation brings together people from different functions with different levels of expertise to work together agrees with past studies that describe skill differentiated teams as cross-functional teams (Hollenbeck et al.,2012; Bell, Brown, Colaneri, & Outland, 2018).

However, the main difference between the findings from this study and past literature is the emphasis on skill differentiation in DevOps teams and how it influences the dimensions of team social capital to form team synergy. The study revealed that skill differentiation promotes synergy between development and IT operations teams through elements that build the dimensions of team social capital such as collaboration, trust, knowledge sharing, and team coordination. Previous studies demonstrated the importance of skill differentiation in the performance of DevOps teams (Zheng, 2012; Wiedemann, & Wiesche, 2018) but the current findings shed more light on how skills differentiations contribute to better team relationships, trust, and knowledge sharing, which promotes the dimensions of team social capital and team synergy. Hence, the results of this study indicate that skill differentiation promote team synergy between development and operations teams in a DevOps environment.

5.1.5 Social Skills

The findings revealed that social skills promote synergy between the development and IT operations teams. Social skills include the ability and willingness to share, communicate and interact with other team members. This is in line with past studies that indicate that social skills allow team members to collaborate and develop better working relationships among team members (Wagner et al., 2014; Wiedemann & Wiesche, 2018). Social skills foster a good working relationship among DevOps teams and mutual trust, knowledge sharing, and willingness to learn from each other are some of the fundamental competences (Wiedemann et al., 2019). However, this study further demonstrated that social skills are necessary to establish and maintain interpersonal relationships among DevOps team members and that these skills promote the dimensions of team social capital and team synergy. While technical skills are also required for team members to accomplish their work, this study revealed that social skills, which include the ability and willingness to share, communicate and interact with other team members are essential in promoting the elements that enable the dimensions of team social capital, which lead to team synergy.

The emphasis of social skills referred to in literature is related to the social competencies required in the DevOps environment (Matook & Maruping, 2014; de França et al., 2016; Wiedemann & Wiesche, 2018; Przybilla et al., 2018; Wiedemann et al., 2019). A noticeable difference in the results of this study, compared to existing literature is the emphasis on the impact of social skills on the dimensions of team social capital and the synergy between development and operation teams. Consequently, the results of this study indicated that social skills promote team synergy between development and operations teams in a DevOps environment.

5.1.6 Mentoring Skills

The study found that mentoring skills are essential to promote team synergy through knowledge sharing. As team members learn and upskill themselves through guidance from the experienced team members, this builds better cross-functional team relationships, and trust, known to be elements that support the dimensions of team social capital. The findings of this study are consistent with previous studies that discuss the expectations of taking responsibility for other team members by mentoring them to develop new knowledge, skills, and capabilities. (Hussain et al., 2017). Mentoring allows DevOps team members to build the skills they need to perform their work effectively through learning and coaching from more experienced members. Shahin, Zahedi, Babar, and Zhu (2017) explained that mentoring skills simplify the process of sharing or shifting operational responsibilities from infrastructure and operations teams to the development team and vice-versa. While the study of Shahin et al. (2017) discussed that mentoring skills allow development and operations team members to mentor, coach, and help each other understand the DevOps environment, by doing so, the findings revealed that mentoring promotes team synergy. When development and operations team members interact and exchange knowledge by mentoring each other, development team members will be able to address operational aspects like deploying and handling incidents in a production environment and vice-versa. Previous studies also emphasized that mentoring skills allow team members to share their experiences, skills, and knowledge, hence allowing them to bridge the gap between development and IT operations (Nielsen, Winkler, & Nørbjerg, 2017). But this study found that such interaction between the DevOps team members further promotes team synergy.

5.1.7 Team Engagement Skills

According to Guchait (2016), team engagement describes the extent to which team members are collectively involved in performing collaborative tasks, and are emotionally connected with each other's task. According to the findings, team engagement skills promote synergy between development and IT operations teams through their interaction and commitment to work together as one team. The findings of this study further revealed that team engagement skills help DevOps team members to build trust, share task-related information and knowledge, and be able to solve complex problems and blockages together. Zoltan (2012) and Rawandi (2009) also confirmed that team engagement leads to the formation of team synergy and they found that teams that have members with a high-level of engagement are more committed in delivering their work as a team. Team engagement reflects team synergy, and team members are cognitively vigilant (Zoltan, 2012). Although scholars have proposed the concept of team engagement, there is a lack of literature supporting how team engagement promotes team synergy in a DevOps environment.

5.1.8 Shared Leadership responsibilities

Shared leadership involves the distribution of leadership responsibilities to multiple team members, and the members perform management duties by motivating other members, giving feedback, and overseeing team tasks (Daspit, Tillman, Boyd, & Mckee, 2013). The emphasis on the importance of shared leadership in software development teams has been widely covered in literature, citing that shared leadership responsibilities bring about team effectiveness (Daspit et al., 2013). In this study, the emphasis of shared leadership responsibilities was primarily on the influence it has on team synergy between the development and IT operations teams. The study revealed that shared leadership responsibilities create an environment that brings development and operations out of silos, hence promoting the dimensions of team social capital and team synergy. That is, shared leadership responsibilities enforce team collaboration, and information is shared openly, and team members take full responsibility for the whole.

The findings of this study also revealed the relevance of shared leadership responsibilities in promoting close team relationships and help development and operations to collaborate and communicate to seek the best solutions and ideas and ensure the quality of service, reliability, and stability of the production system. Consistent with Harvard Business Review, collaborative leadership promotes a diversity of opinions and ideas among team members to formulate strategies and solve problems (Ibarra & Hansen, 2011). Therefore, with shared leadership, DevOps team members are more engaged, feel trusted, and are more likely to take ownership of their work (White, 2019). These are similar to the findings of this study, which pointed out that when development and operations teams work together and share leadership responsibilities throughout the DevOps life cycle, they develop team better relationships and promote team ownership. However, this current study further demonstrated that team ownership through shared leadership responsibilities improve the dimensions of team social capital, which in turn promotes team synergy between the development and IT operations teams.

5.1.9 Shared Decision Making

The study found that shared decision-making leads to better team synergy through open communication and interaction between development and operations teams to make collective decisions that best suit the norms of the DevOps teams. While investigating IT governance mechanisms for DevOps oriented IT functions, Wiedemann (2018) found that organizations with DevOps oriented teams promote autonomy in their decision-making processes. Both development and operations team members are involved in the decision-making process. The outcome of this study emphasizes that DevOps team members are all allowed to make decisions relating to planning, tests, and monitoring which is consistent with previous studies (Wiedemann et al.,2019; Wiedemann, 2018).

DevOps oriented teams participate in decision-making processes team members feel responsible and have a sense of ownership of the service relevant activities. (Wiedemann & Schulz, 2017). Both literature and the findings revealed that shared decision-making promotes better communication, collaboration, and knowledge sharing. However, the results of this study extend to what is in the literature by emphasizing that shared decision-making promotes the dimensions of team social capital and team synergy through better communication, collaboration, and knowledge sharing. The emphasis on the importance of shared decision making in promoting team synergy between development and IT operations teams in the findings of this study addresses existing gaps with the previous studies.

5.1.10 Choice of Technology

According to the findings, the choice of technologies depends on the extent to which the technology supports DevOps functions, for instance, better collaboration, communication, build automation, repositories management, and deployments. The study revealed that these functions are essential in promoting team synergy between the development and operations teams. The study of Airaj (2017) supports that tools and technologies provide DevOps teams with capability for versioning, build and packaging, continuous integration, virtual infrastructure, configuration management, orchestration and application deployment, and monitoring. These functions allow development and operations personnel to interact, collaborate, coordinate, and communicate their work activities (Erich, 2018). Choosing the right tools influences the success of DevOps teams and the effectiveness of DevOps practices (Bou Ghantous & Gill, 2017; Shahin et al., 2017; Bucena, & Kirikova, 2017).

On the other hand, the findings of this study are consistent with the previous studies that indicate that due to the wide variety of available options conflicts may arise between the DevOps team members while choosing the right tools (Wettinger, Andrikopoulos, & Leymann, 2015; Gill et al., 2018; Bheri & Vummenthala, 2019). Section 5.2.15 of this study discusses how these challenges inhibit the dimensions of team social capital and prevent the synergy between the development and operations teams.

5.1.11 Willingness to Share Information

The study revealed that willingness to share information has a positive influence on team synergy. According to the findings, when DevOps team members share information openly, a common understanding of the task or activity is built, which also encourages the DevOps team members to collaborate. As a result, it promotes relational and cognitive dimensions of team social capital, which leads to synergy.

While Wiedemann et al. (2019) explained that sharing information and knowledge provides fundamental knowledge to support, manage, and integrate DevOps services across the teams, the findings of this study emphasized that willingness to share information contributes to the dimensions of team social capital to promote team synergy. Previous studies commonly cited the importance of knowledge sharing in promoting social interaction between DevOps teams (Horlach et al., 2017; Nielsen et al., 2017), as one of the essential dimensions of DevOps (Lwakatare et al., 2015) that provide learning opportunities to other DevOps team members (Weiedemann & Wiesche, 2018). In line with past studies, the findings also emphasise that knowledge sharing and willingness to share information contribute towards the success of DevOps teams. However, the results of this study further highlight how willingness to share information contribute towards the dimensions of team social capital through knowledge sharing, collaboration, and interaction between the development and IT operations teams, which promote synergy.

5.1.12 Organizational Culture

The findings revealed that an organizational culture values team collaboration promotes team synergy between the development and IT operations. The literature maintains that when an organizational culture integrates people and ideas to support people inside the organization structure, it positively influences trust and the flow of information among DevOps teams (Forsgren & Humble, 2016; Colomo-Palacios et al., 2018). Furthermore, reports on the state of DevOps (Forsgren et al., 2014) and previous studies (Humble, & Molesky, 2011; Bang, Chung, Choy, & Dupuis, 2013) emphasized the importance of organizational culture in building better team relationships between development and IT operations teams. In line with the previous studies, the findings also revealed that when the organization culture supports change, teams find it easier to adopt the same mindset shift.

A culture where teams share common values is difficult to achieve when development and IT operations teams are integrated without aligning the organization culture with a DevOps culture. (Walls, 2013). The DevOps paradigm introduces a change in organizational culture to promote collaboration, automation, sharing, continuous integration, and delivery software (Rajkumar et al., 2016; Forsgren & Humble, 2016; Wiedemann, 2018). In line with the previous studies, the findings also highlighted that DevOps is a cultural shift, not at team level but the organization as a whole. In turn, that promotes team synergy between the development and IT operations teams through collaboration, common values and sharing.

This study is consistent with the literature that discusses the impact of cultural differences as impediments that introduce friction between development and operations teams (Farroha & Farroha, 2014; Lwakatare et al., 2015; Gill at al., 2018). Hence, it is plausible that development and operations teams may have different predispositions, experiences, and biases towards DevOps processes. The difference in the findings of this study, as compared to existing literature, was the emphasis on how cultural differences in an organization, can also impair the elements that form the dimensions of team social capital, for example, trust, collaborations, and knowledge sharing. These will be further discussed in the next section.

5.2 Factors That Prevent Team Synergy

5.2.1 Organisation Culture

As highlighted in section 5.1.12, the study revealed that organizational culture could promote or prevent team synergy. On the negative side, the study revealed that an organizational culture that does not support a DevOps culture prevents team synergy between development and operations teams. Furthermore, this study pointed out that cultural differences lead to team conflicts, which in turn cause breakdown in trust, coordination, and collaboration among

DevOps team members. This in turn, inhibit the three dimensions of team social capital and team synergy. According to the IBM Solutions and I.T. Infrastructure, teams consist of people, each with unique inclinations, experiences, and biases, which makes it difficult to exhibit a common organizational culture. The results of this study emphasized that these cultural differences potentially create conflicts between the teams, which makes it challenging to achieve team synergy between the development and operations teams.

Davis and Daniels (2016) found that there are common misconceptions about DevOps within organizations leading teams to confuse the definition of DevOps and unable to articulate the expectations and value DevOps brings to the organization. DevOps anti-patterns (misconceptions and distortions about the concept) have led to incorrect restructuring for DevOps teams (Sharma, 2017), for example, a new leadership role (Dev and Ops reporting to one manager), new silos, and teams with only Dev and Ops practitioners. While these anti-patterns may tend to resolve a few problems, they can still maintain siloed units that did not change, therefore they are not closer to having better communication, collaboration, and trust. This study positions the organization as the main driver for cultural change, citing that the organization can either play a supporting or neglecting role towards cultural change. Furthermore, the results of this study suggested that changing the way development and operations teams work to achieve team synergy requires a change in culture and should be driven by the organization's culture.

5.2.2 Challenges Associated with DevOps Processes and Tools

The study revealed that challenges that are associated with DevOps processes and tools prevent synergy between development and operations teams. According to the findings these challenges were identified as expired licenses and service plan, and storage space issues, limited support for DevOps practices and counter-productive processes. This study's results agree with the existing literature that indicates that commercial and expensive proprietary tools are prohibitive to the work of DevOps teams, for instance, limiting deployment options within organizations (Birngruber, Forai, & Zauner, 2015). In this study, these proprietary tools that have different licensing plans, were regarded as very expensive to accommodate all the DevOps team members and prevented the teams from working together with the same tooling. Sometimes, the teams had to deal with expired licenses and service plans. Therefore, being closed source, the functionality of the tools cannot be reused or extended due to the license agreements (Brunnert et al.,2015). This study emphasized that expired licenses and service plans inhibit the dimensions of team social and then team synergy between development and operations teams since they are unable to work collaboratively while using the same tools. DevOps team members depend on the uninterrupted availability of infrastructure, licenses, and connectivity to meet individual milestones (Patwardhan, 2017).

In terms of challenges relating to the support of DevOps practices through processes and tools, the literature revealed that there are still tools with limited support for DevOps practices. Examples include, lack of proper automation tools to continuously deploy new software features into the production environment (Hamunen, 2016; Amaradri & Nutalapati, 2016;

Lwakatare et al., 2016; Bucena & Kirikova, 2017). As a result. Claps et al. (2015) noted potential team challenges when deploying software frequently without automation tools, for instance, operations team members blaming development for introducing bugs and causing instability in the production environment. This study found that lack of automation features in some of the processes and tools impairs the dimensions of team social capital and prevents team synergy between the DevOps teams when team members start to blame each for introducing errors into the production environment. While the results of this study are consistent with previous studies regarding the challenges arising from limitations within DevOps tools and processes (Humble and Farley, 2010; Lwakatare et al., 2015), the results of this study emphasized the negative impact of these challenges on development and operations team synergy.

Furthermore, the study revealed that DevOps processes still integrate ITIL processes, which are counter-productive to DevOps teams. The processes are characterized by long administrative and silo driven processes, which hinder team synergy between the development and IT operations teams. These processes strive to handle the volume of changes, and the speed of development DevOps can bring to the organization (Hamunen, 2016). This study found that the processes that have long administrative procedures have a negative impact on team engagement, communication, team coordination, and team collaboration. The results of this study emphasized that counterproductive processes inhibit the dimensions of team social capital and prevent team synergy between development and operations teams.

5.2.3 Resistance to Change

The findings revealed that resistance to change gives rise to limited cooperation and a lack of trust among the DevOps teams, which prevents team synergy between development and IT operations teams. Researchers indicate that resistance to change is one of the common challenges facing teams when adopting DevOps practices and is known to sabotage new ideas and thoughts (Wurster, Colville, Haight, Tripathi, & Rastogi, 2013). It may often be the case that the development and operations teams have conflicting goals (Hüttermann, 2012). In addition, this study also found that operations team often assume that changes from the development team are often disruptive and render the production environment less stable. The previous studies highlighted that resistance to change is one of the challenges facing DevOps teams. Other researchers suggested that communicating how the change will benefit the organization and the employees individually might help to deal with resistance (Hussaini, 2014; Prakash, & Moharir, 2019).

This study is consistent with the literature that indicates that resistance to change may give rise to a lack of team-level support, team awareness, or team members to fear that their jobs may be affected (Bucena & Kirikova, 2017). However, one exception is that the results of this study emphasized that the identified factors inhibit the dimensions of team social capital, which in turn prevent development and operations from achieving team synergy. Further investigation is needed to identify strategies that can be applied to improve on these factors will help DevOps teams to overcome resistance and to achieve team synergy.

5.2.4 Poor Staff retention and job security

According to the findings, poor staff retention and job security result to a feeling of uncertainty, low morale, lack of trust, and reduced participation from team members, which inhibits the dimensions of team social capital and prevents team synergy. The study of Shropshire and Sweeney (2017) on DevOps and Workforce Morale explains that team members' morale is manifested in terms of perceived organizational support, job satisfaction, affective commitment, leader consideration, and perceived fairness. The authors revealed that decreased morale leads to reduced employee performance. The emphasis on poor staff retention and job security in this study is consistent with past studies regarding team members' morale and commitment. While the results of this study indicate that job security increases team members' commitment and team participation, some team members who are contractors might not know the fate of their contracts. Contract negotiations may lead to job insecurity (Van den Broeck et al., 2014), which prevents team participation, engagement, and low morale. According to this study, team members may feel disengage when employment conditions are not favorable and see their employment as temporary until they move on to the next job. This study found that these conditions prevents interaction, positive communication and the hoarding of work-related information between team members which negatively affect the dimensions of team social capital and team synergy between development and operations teams.

The results of this study also concluded that conflicts between in-house and outsourced team members pay less attention not only the principles of DevOps but also the dimensions of team social capital, which prevent team synergy. Liu and Yuliani (2016) found that outsourcing project team members result in conflicting goals between outsourced and in-house team members, which subsequently affects the willingness of the team members to contribute to knowledge sharing. While the findings of this study demonstrated that conflicts between the contractors and permanent staff exhibit the "us" versus "them" mentality among the DevOps team members. While the conflicts between in-house and outsourced are well known in software development teams research in general, the findings of this study revealed that these conflicts also exist in DevOps teams. Therefore, it is another area this study extends to the existing literature, including emphasizing that poor staff retention and job security prevent the synergy between development and operations teams.

5.2.5 Poor Work-life balance

The study revealed that poor work-life balance leads to work-related pressure, which negatively affects team morale, mood, behavior, and performance. The previous section the study emphasized the impact of low morale to the dimensions of team social capital and team synergy. The findings of this study regarding poor work-life balance are closely aligned with the existing literature, which explained that excessive workload gives rise to poor teamwork, poor morale, and burnout (Davis & Daniels, 2016). However, this study gave more emphasis on the impact of poor work-life on the dimensions of team social capital and team synergy between the development and operations teams. DevOps is about creating sustainable work practices, and how individuals approach their work-life balance is an essential part (Davis & Daniels, 2016). However, this study revealed that the nature of DevOps work requires team members to collaborate regularly during evenings and weekends. In this study, the issue of limited skills and experience on some of the team members result in urgent work being given to the experienced team members. Therefore, some team members end up with an excessive workload. While this exposes an element of poor knowledge sharing, the researcher felt there is a need to implement strategies to upskill the less experienced team members.

The results of this study are consistent with previous studies, which found that the work carried out by development and operations teams has traditionally required them to work outside working hours (Forsgren & Humble, 2016). The nature of work is either maintenance on-call or non-standard shifts to provide 24/7 coverage (Bastarrica, Espinoza, & Marín, 2018). It is necessary to keep in mind that these kinds of requirements can be unintentionally disadvantages team members. Hence, the results of this study together with previous studies that indicate that the work-life balance for team members working in these conditions is not sustainable, and burn out does happen (Swartout, 2018; Forsgren & Humble, 2016). On the other hand, this study demonstrated how the impact of poor work-life balance on the dimensions of team social capital and prevent the synergy between development and operations team members.

5.2.6 Lack of investment in DevOps

The study revealed that lack of investment in DevOps prevent team synergy between development and IT operations teams. Insufficient resources, training, and limited tools lead to limited collaboration and exchange of information among the DevOps teams, making it difficult for the development and operations team to coordinate their work effectively. Literature also indicates that there is a need to invest in proper DevOps tools, infrastructure, and training to improve the skills of DevOps team members (Bucena & Kirikova, 2017; Chen, 2018; Prakash & Moharir, 2019). The results of this study agree with the literature on the importance of investing in DevOps and advising that investment in DevOps skills, infrastructure. However, this study found that a lack of investment limits DevOps teams from achieving their goals, which include team collaboration, knowledge sharing, and effective coordination of tasks, regarded as elements that form the dimensions of team social capital and then team synergy.

Past studies that discussed the failure or success of DevOps teams emphasized that investment in IT infrastructure and resources is a critical prerequisite for the success of DevOps teams (Ikerionwu, & Edgar, 2016). Moreover, Kamuto and Langerman (2017) explained that lack of investment in DevOps may result in unresolved barriers between the development and operations. This study emphasized that lack of investment in DevOps not only leads to unresolved barriers but also prevents the synergy between development and operations teams by inhibiting the dimensions of team social capital. Based on the results of this study, it might be relevant for management to invest in the necessary tools, resources, and training to improve the quality of service and the expertise of team members in implementing DevOps practices It will also improve team collaboration, knowledge sharing, and efficiency in task coordination, which are elements supporting the dimensions of team social capital.

5.2.7 Lack of Management Involvement

The study revealed that lack of management involvement leads to conditions that impair synergy between the development and operations teams. Involvement can be described as the extent to which management is involved in providing all the necessary support team members require to execute their work effectively (De Brentani, Kleinschmidt, & Salomo, 2010). While the adoption of DevOps requires strong management support and buy-in to succeed, Hamunen (2016) revealed that the lack of management involvement is still a known challenge. Because DevOps has to do with numerous changes in the way different teams are working daily, a high commitment and support at the top level of the organization is necessary to change the company culture. According to Riungu-Kalliosaari et al. (2016), the role of management involvement is to help development and operations teams break down the walls and allocate more time for communication and sharing. Therefore, it is challenging to successfully adopt a DevOps culture when there is limited involvement from management (Jones, Noppen, & Lettice, 2016). The previous studies maintained that lack of management is one of the challenges DevOps teams are facing when adopting DevOps. However, the results of this study pointed out how lack of management involvement negatively affects the dimensions of team social capital and prevents the synergy between development and operations teams.

5.2.8 Job descriptions

The study revealed that job descriptions usually promote development and operations teams to function in isolation, making it difficult for the teams to work towards a common goal. This further prevents team synergy between development and operations teams. Nybom et al., 2015) found that mixing the responsibilities between development and operations leads to an eye-opening experience, collaborative ways of working, and improved collaboration. On the other hand, their study raised concerns with mixing responsibilities citing that people are more comfortable with what they are used to doing and found it challenging to introduce operations tasks to development. This study found those team members who are fixed roles and responsibilities limit themselves from interacting with other team members, learning opportunities, and sharing task-related information. While the previous studies highlighted the impact of mixing the responsibilities between development and operations teams, none of that discussed how it could directly affect team synergy. The results of this study then emphasized that strict adherence to fixed roles and responsibilities impede DevOps teams from achieving the dimensions of team social capital and prevent team synergy.

The results of this study are consistent with the existing literature that indicates that development team members doing operations tasks could lead to negative team experience (Dyck et al., 2015; Nybom et al., 2016; Hussain et al., 2017). This study indicated that performing beyond the stipulated job description could lead to inappropriate and undermining behaviors, which could potentially affect the dimensions of team social capital negatively. The thought of overstepping boundaries from team members could negatively affect team relationships.

5.2.9 Organizational bureaucracy

The study revealed that some of the regulatory processes become over-bureaucratic, restricting the development and operations teams from coordinating their tasks effectively and prevent team synergy. Many studies showed that bureaucratic processes negatively affects DevOps practices, team structures, collaboration, and responsibilities (van Ommeren, van Doorn, Dial, & van Herpes, 2018; Shahin., 2015; Agarwal, Gupta, & Choudhury, 2018). Shahin et al. (2017) found that deployment processes in some organizations are still highly bureaucratic. While their findings described bureaucratic processes as formalized manual tasks that are executed before each release and having a chain of people to approve each step, this study emphasized the impact of organizational bureaucracy on team synergy. Bureaucracy does not adapt to change faster (Alvares & Schwartz, 2019). This study's results emphasized that organizational bureaucracy prevents team synergy between the development and operations teams because of the delays and frustrations it injects within the DevOps processes. Furthermore, this study highlighted that these delays break the team spirit and agility expected of a DevOps environment and making it unfeasible for the teams to communicate, coordinate, and deliver their work faster. In this study, communication and coordination were considered essential elements that contribute to the dimensions of team social capital, which lead to team synergy.

According to Rance (2011), many IT organizations still include regular Change Advisory Board (CAB) meetings in their DevOps, where changes are discussed, and decisions are made about which changes will be implemented. While the function of the Change Advisory Board enforces change controls in the software development process, this study highlights that the documentation and endless series of reviews and checks the CAB expects slows down the whole DevOps deployment process. Consequently, this study found the CAB as an impediment to the exchange of knowledge and communication, which inhibits the dimensions of team social capital and prevents team synergy among development and operations teams. There is a need to explore better strategies to ensure these bureaucratic processes align with a DevOps culture, where agility and team synergy are more prioritized.

5.2.10 Counter-productive Change Control Processes

The study revealed that counter-productive change control processes negatively impact team synergy as they tend to prolong the DevOps life cycle and feedback loops. Delays in feedback give rise to misalignment of goals between the teams and slow down the exchange of task-related information and knowledge among the DevOps team members. De França et al. (2016) explained that counter-productive tools and processes affect the level of flexibility and creativity among team members. Several studies agree that flexibility and creativity have a direct influence on the dimensions of team social capital (Li & Maedche, 2012; Wiedemann & Weeger, 2017). The findings of this study emphasized that a lack of flexibility and creativity within the change control processes negatively influences team synergy between development and IT operations. This study found that counter-productive change control processes are still prevalent in some DevOps processes yet they do not align well with the cross-functional nature of DevOps (Ravichandran et al., 2016). The results of this study found that traditional change controls introduce delays in DevOps processes and unnecessary hinderances to team collaboration This study agrees with the previous studies that indicate that many organizations still have traditional ITIL change management processes merged into their DevOps practices (Phifer, 2011; Rance, 2011; Cao & Zhang, 2016). These processes were designed when plan-driven approaches were still in use, and there was less demand for frequent releases. This study found that these processes are no longer coping well with the present demand for frequent deployments the DevOps teams expect. Previous studies indicate that the application of counter-productive processes in DevOps environments could cause delays in the software delivery process, which leads to low team morale and frustration (Matook & Maruping, 2014; Ravichandran et al.,2016). The results of this study extended to the previous studies by emphasizing that counter-productive change control processes prevent the development and IT operations from achieving team synergy and struggles to develop a comprehensive DevOps culture.

This study revealed that counterproductive change control processes are ineffective as they prolong DevOps life cycle times and feedback loops, which negatively impacts the dimensions of team social capital and prevent team synergy between development and operations teams. The difference in the results of this study compared to the previous studies was the emphasis on the impact of counterproductive change controls processes on the synergy between development and operations synergy in this study.

5.2.11 Organisation restructuring

According to the findings, organization restructuring disrupts the existing DevOps team structures and their social ties, causing a breakdown to the existing synergy between development and operations teams. While Shropshire and Sweeney (2017) indicated that changes in the organization structure lead to some degree of fear and skepticism, and a reduction in team morale, this study emphasized that restructuring involving staff retrenchments or voluntary retirement creates skills and knowledge gaps within DevOps teams. However, this study agree with Shropshire and Sweeney on that restructuring leads to low team morale, in the sense that when people leave the organization not only do they go with their skills, knowledge and experience but also leave more work responsibilities (excessive workload) to the remaining staff. This study emphasised that low team morale negatively affect the dimensions of team social capital, hence prevents the synergy between development and operations teams.

5.2.12 Lack of experienced leadership

The findings revealed that a lack of experienced leadership leads to a lack of direction, coordination, and loss of morale, which prevents team synergy between the development and IT operations teams. While DevOps culture involves creating new shared values and behaviors across IT teams, it is challenging to drive and achieve these characteristics across the entire organization with inexperienced leaders (Ravichandran et al. (2016). The results of this study are consistent with existing literature, which indicates that a lack of experienced leadership is one of the challenges facing DevOps teams (Scekic, Gazivoda, Scepanovic, & Nikolic, 2018; Wiedemann et al., 2019). On the other hand, the findings of this study demonstrated that a lack of experienced steers DevOps team in the wrong direction and could lead to challenges that impair the dimensions of team social capital and prevent the synergy between development and operations teams. The results of this study pointed out that silos across the organization, ineffective lines of communication, low team morale, insecurity, limited management involvement, and lack of team engagement are effects of incompetent leadership, which impede the dimensions of team social capital, and prevents team synergy.

The results of this study also revealed that the need for strong and experienced leadership is not that important since in a DevOps environment leadership is shared among team members. The preferred leadership style in a DevOps environment is where team members organise themselves and share leadership responsibilities relates to the same approach used in Agile teams (Tanner, & von Willingh, 2014). This study earlier noted that shared leadership improves the dimensions of team social capital and team synergy. Consequently, DevOps teams that are experiencing leadership and synergy challenges can transform their management style.

5.2.13 Challenges of Using technology

Although the study revealed that technology enables DevOps team members to work better and faster, there were noted challenges encountered when using technology. These challenges are lack of collaboration features in some of the tools, resistance to use certain technologies, and limited knowledge and understanding of the technology. Past studies also indicates that challenges using technology includes worries on how to choose the right tools and integrate them with existing tools and practices (Bucena, & Kirikova, 2017; Aljundi, 2018). DevOps teams depend on these tools during continuous integration, and continuous deployment, therefore, choosing the right set of tools enable efficient delivery of their work.

The emphasis on the challenges faced by DevOps teams in choosing the right tools is consistent with existing literature relating to the adoption of DevOps. Amaradri and Nutalapati (2016) maintained that the organization is responsible for deciding which tools and technologies to adopt, but the challenge they face is an unawareness of the right tools for certain tasks. In this study, unawareness of the right DevOps potentially creates problems where the DevOps teams end up with tools and technologies that have limited support for DevOps. The toolset required for DevOps is particularly diverse and finding the right fit, correct usage and attitudes towards that technology is challenging (Hamunen, 2016; Bucena & Kirikova, 2017). This study also found that the availability of many DevOps tools on the market, present challenges for team members in selecting the tools they all like. Some of the challenges revealed in this study were little understanding of the tools, lack of trust, and conflicting views on choosing the right tools, which impairs the dimensions of team social capital and team synergy.

5.2.14 Complex technical infrastructure

The study revealed that a complex technical infrastructure introduces challenges such as poor coordination and limited knowledge sharing that negatively affect team relationships leading to impaired dimensions of team social capital, therefore preventing team synergy between the development and operations teams. According to Wiedemann et al. (2019), the complexity of the DevOps technical infrastructure requires team members to have all-rounded skills. However, due to a shortage of skills, most teams are still learning. This study found that there is a need for DevOps team members to have the skills necessary to understand the technical infrastructure and work effectively with others. Consequently, the results of this study emphasized that complex technical infrastructure introduces challenges that negatively affect the relationships among the DevOps teams, inhibiting the dimensions of team social, and prevent team synergy.

The findings of this study showed that team members consume a lot of time trying to understand the technical infrastructure. As a result, it leads to poor coordination of tasks and limited sharing of task-related information and knowledge between development and operations teams. These findings are consistent with the previous studies that indicate that a team without the expertise and knowledge needed to deal with complex situations leads to delays in achieving its goals, coordination breakdowns, and delayed feedback (Banica, Radulescu, Rosca, & Hagiu, 2017; Hagemann & Kluge, 2017). While the findings of this study are consistent with the existing literature regarding the challenges DevOps teams are facing working in complex environment, the results of this study go beyond the challenges to discuss the impact of these challenges to the dimensions of team social capital and team synergy. This study found that the complex technical infrastructure prevent the synergy between development and operations teams.

5.3 Summary

In this chapter, the research phenomenon, the research objectives, research purpose and research questions have been addressed. The exploration into the factors that influence team synergy between development and IT operations teams in a DevOps environment has exposed the state of DevOps from a literature perspective as well as the practitioners' viewpoint. The conceptual model for team social capital as the basis for team synergy (Zoltan, 2012) been extended to reflect the findings from the study.

Recognizing that DevOps teams face several challenges, the factors identified in this study will give insights into how organizations can influence the build and motivate their DevOps teams to achieve team synergy. Furthermore, the results contribute to research and the industry by helping to understand the factors that influence the team synergy in a DevOps environment. The next chapter concludes with recommendations and suggestions for further research.

Chapter 6: Conclusion

This chapter concludes the research, by re-stating the study objectives, and what was achieved in each case. The chapter also states the research contributions, limitations, and suggestions for future research.

6.1 Summary of Research Objectives

When teams collaborate, organizations can respond quickly to the rapidly changing environment. However, it is a challenge to get teams to work together efficiently and effectively to achieve common goals. Many organizations have adopted DevOps to promote effective team collaboration and communication between the development and operations teams, which incited the need for team synergy among these teams. Team synergy provides more capacity for development teams to cooperate, be supportive, collaborative, be helpful, and mutually learn from each other, which is associated with modern software development practices such as DevOps. This study investigated the factors that influenced team synergy between the development and operations teams in a DevOps environment, which prompts the objectives of the study.

The objectives of the study were as follows:

1. To identify the factors that influence the synergy between development and IT operations within a DevOps environment.

2. To identify which one of the factors identified promote the synergy between development and IT operations.

3. To identify which one of the factors identified inhibit the synergy between development and IT operations.

6.2 Summary of Findings

The overall purpose of this study was to identify the factors that influence the synergy between development and operations teams in a DevOps environment. The factors were summarized based on the research questions. To answer the research questions, the study identified and classified the factors that influence the synergy between development and operations teams in a DevOps environment. In line with the research questions, the factors identified were grouped into two categories, which are enabling (see Table 6.2) and inhibiting factors (see Table 6.3).

- **Enabling Factors (see Table 6.2)**

Enabling factors were identified as factors that promote the dimensions of team social capital and team synergy between the development and operations teams. These were classified as organizational, task characteristics, team processes, use of technology and knowledge sharing. The findings highlighted essential elements, such as collaboration, trust, coordination, knowledge sharing, etc. that make up the dimensions of team social capital. By highlighting these factors, the findings were able to respond to the question: What factors are enablers of relational, structural and cognitive dimensions of social capital as a basis for team synergy between development and IT operations?

Table 6.2: Factors that promote team synergy

Organisational Factors
Management Initiatives to promote DevOps teams
Organisational Culture
Task Characteristics
Nature of work
Good Management of Task dependencies
Knowledge Skills and Abilities
Skills Differentiation
Team Processes
Shared leadership responsibilities
Shared decision making
Management and Team Leads
Use of Technology
Choice of Technology
Knowledge Sharing
Information Shared
Willingness to share information and knowledge

- **Inhibiting Factors (see Table 6.3)**

The study found these factors as inhibitors to the desired dimensions of team social capital, which prevents team synergy between the development and operations. These factors were classified as environmental, organizational, team processes, and challenges related to the use of technology in a DevOps environment. To improve team synergy, DevOps teams should address issues around these factors.

Table 6.3: Factors that inhibit team synergy

Environmental Factors
Complex technical infrastructure
Challenges associated with DevOps processes and tools
Resistance to change
Poor Staff retention and job security
Poor Lack of work-life balance
Organisational Factors
Lack of investment in DevOps
Lack of management involvement
Job descriptions
Separated DevOps teams
Organizational bureaucracy
Counter-productive Change control Processes
Organisation Restructuring
Organisation Culture
Team Processes
Lack of experienced leadership
Use of Technology
Challenges of using technology

6.3 Research Contribution

The following section describes how the contributions are beneficial to practice and future researchers. The study contributes to the body of knowledge through a theoretical framework which includes the factors that influence the synergy between development and operations teams in a DevOps environment. The theoretical framework depicted the factors that promote and prevent team synergy and to explain the significance of team social capital dimensions in the formation or achievement of team synergy.

To date, a considerable body of research has sought to understand DevOps, its benefits and challenges faced during its implementation and adoption. This research provides several valuable insights, especially towards the conditions that influence team synergy within DevOps teams. The study's emphasis on the importance of team synergy and team social capital towards team performance and effectiveness will add value to DevOps teams and the way things are done in DevOps environments. Also, by highlighting the factors that influence on the synergy between development and operations teams in a DevOps environment is a contribution to knowledge that can be used to smoothen the DevOps adoption process. The factors highlighted in the findings can be used as a reference of important aspects that need constant monitoring.

The results from these findings could help the practitioners and organizations to have a clear understanding of which factors that reduce or increase team performance in a DevOps environment. The findings will also add value and provide organizations an opportunity to improve on areas that they find impeding the desired team synergy. The knowledge accumulated in this study on the factors that promote the dimensions of team social capital will assist organizations that have adopted DevOps and those still planning to implement DevOps in achieving team synergy.

6.4 Limitations of the Study

The data collection process and methods were also the limitations of this study. This study was conducted in a real-world setting, the data collected through interviews, participant observation, and review documents. Therefore, the validity and credibility of the study depended on the input provided by the participants interviewed and certain areas the researcher granted access to observe. The information accumulated depended on what the participants were willing to share, limited to their perspective and experiences regarding DevOps. Moreover, people act in a certain way when they know they are being observed. However, the triangulation of data in this study helped in the validation and verification of the results.

6.5 Future Research

Based on the limitations that were identified in section 6.4, it is possible to highlight areas or gaps for future research. First, areas for future research that were not taken into the scope of this study are identified. Next, associated research questions for possible future research are presented.

The primary objective of the study was to identify the factors that influence team synergy between development and IT operations teams in a DevOps environment. The study identified the factors that promote and prevent team synergy within DevOps teams but did not order the identified factors in their order of importance. Ordering the factors with their degree of influence could provide better insights into organizations and their DevOps teams.

In addition, DevOps appears to operate in a complex and dynamic environment with many stakeholders and complex technical infrastructure. Based on this finding, another research study could be taken with a focus on the system thinking approach. A soft systems methodology would create a different perspective on the synergy between DevOps teams by focusing on the behavior of the actors and complex problematic situations involving social activities. Such research could investigate the influence of different elements in the organization related to DevOps team synergy and better team performance. Knowing the influence of multiple elements on the system and its environment can be an addition to this research in order to increase the knowledge on the adoption of DevOps.

The study identified the factors that promote and prevent team synergy within DevOps teams but did not suggest strategies to mitigate the factors that prevent team synergy. Future studies could further investigate and develop strategies to mitigate the factors that inhibit the dimensions of team social capital and prevent team synergy in a DevOps environment. A recommended future study will be to take the factors identified and conduct a statistical factor analysis, such as confirmatory factor analysis, to verify and solidify this study. It will help confirm and verify the hypothesized theoretical framework. Also, confirm whether the factors identified fit well with data.

References

Agarwal, A., Gupta, S., & Choudhury, T. (2018, June). Continuous and Integrated Software Development using DevOps. In 2018 International Conference on Advances in Computing and Communication Engineering (ICACCE) (pp. 290-293). IEEE.

Amaradri, A. S., & Nutalapati, S. B. (2016). Continuous Integration, Deployment and Testing in DevOps Environment.

Anfara Jr, V. A., Brown, K. M., & Mangione, T. L. (2002). Qualitative analysis on stage: Making the research process more public. Educational researcher, 31(7), 28-38.

Airaj, M. (2017). Enable cloud DevOps approach for industry and higher education. Concurrency and Computation: Practice and Experience, 29(5), e3937.

Aljundi, M. K. (2018). Tools and practices to enhance DevOps core values

Alnaji, L., & Salameh, H. (2015). Performance-measurement framework to evaluate software engineers for agile software-development methodology. European Journal of Business and Management, 7(2), 183-190.

Alsharo, M., Gregg, D., & Ramirez, R. (2017). Virtual team effectiveness: The role of knowledge sharing and trust. Information & Management, 54(4), 479-490.

Alvares, S. A., & Schwartz, M. (2019, October 30). Mark Schwartz on DevOps, Bureaucracy and His Upcoming Book at 2019 DevOps Enterprise Summit (DOES). Retrieved from https://www.infoq.com/news/2019/10/devops-bureaucracy/.

Bahari, S. F. (2010). Qualitative versus quantitative research strategies: contrasting epistemological and ontological assumptions. Sains Humanika, 52(1).

Banica, L., Radulescu, M., Rosca, D., & Hagiu, A. (2017). Is DevOps another Project Management Methodology?. Informatica Economica, 21(3), 39.

Bang, S. K., Chung, S., Choy, Y., & Dupuis, M. (2013, October). A grounded theory analysis of modern web applications: knowledge, skills, and abilities for DevOps. In Proceedings of the 2nd annual conference on Research in information technology (pp. 61-62). ACM.

Bass, L., Weber, I., & Zhu, L. (2015). DevOps: A software architect's perspective. Addison-Wesley Professional.

Bastarrica, M. C., Espinoza, G., & Marín, J. (2018, October). Implementing agile practices: the experience of TSol. In Proceedings of the 12th ACM/IEEE International Symposium on Empirical Software Engineering and Measurement (p. 38). ACM.

Baxter, P., & Jack, S. (2008). Qualitative case study methodology: Study design and implementation for novice researchers. The qualitative report, 13(4), 544-559.

Bell, S. T., Brown, S. G., Colaneri, A., & Outland, N. (2018). Team composition and the ABCs of teamwork. American Psychologist, 73(4), 349.

Bhattacherjee, A. (2012). Social science research: Principles, methods, and practices.

Bheri, S., & Vummenthala, S. (2019). An Introduction to the DevOps Tool Related Challenges.

Bierwolf, R., Frijns, P., & van Kemenade, P. (2017, October). Project management in a dynamic environment: Balancing stakeholders. In 2017 IEEE European Technology and Engineering Management Summit (E-TEMS) (pp. 1-6). IEEE.

Birngruber, E., Forai, P., & Zauner, A. (2015, November). Total recall: holistic metrics for broad systems performance and user experience visibility in a data-intensive computing environment. In Proceedings of the Second International Workshop on HPC User Support Tools (p. 5). ACM.

Bou Ghantous, G., & Gill, A. (2017). DevOps: Concepts, Practices, Tools, Benefits and Challenges. PACIS2017.

Boyatzis, R. E. (1998). Transforming qualitative information: Thematic analysis and code development. sage.

Brown, M. (2014). Groupthink in software engineering. International Journal of Computing and Business Research.

Bruel, J. M., & Jiménez, M. (2018, March). DevOps' 18 Education Panel. In International Workshop on   Software Engineering Aspects of Continuous Development and New Paradigms of Software Production and Deployment (pp. 221-226). Springer, Cham.

Brunnert, A., van Hoorn, A., Willnecker, F., Danciu, A., Hasselbring, W., Heger, C., ... & Koziolek, A. (2015). Performance-oriented DevOps: A research agenda. arXiv preprint arXiv:1508.04752.

Braun, V., & Clarke, V. (2006). Using thematic analysis in psychology. Qualitative research in psychology, 3(2), 77-101.

Bryman, A. and Bell, E. (2015) Business research methods. Oxford University Press, USA.

Bucena, I., & Kirikova, M. (2017). Simplifying the DevOps Adoption Process. In BIR Workshops.

Bucero, A., & Englund, R. L. (2015, October). Project sponsorship: Achieving management commitment for project success. Project Management Institute.

Cagle, R., Rice, T., & Kristan, M. (2015). DevOps for federal acquisition. In IEEE Software Technology Conference.

Cao, J. Q., & Zhang, S. H. (2016). ITIL Incident Management Process Reengineering in Industry 4.0 Environments. In Proceedings of the 2nd International Conference on Advances in Mechanical Engineering and Industrial Informatics (AMEII 2016) (Vol. 73, pp. 1011-6).

Carroll, L. S. L. (2017). A Comprehensive Definition of Technology from an Ethological Perspective. Social Sciences, 6(4), 126.

Chan, X. W., Kalliath, T., Brough, P., Siu, O. L., O'Driscoll, M. P., & Timms, C. (2016). Work–family enrichment and satisfaction: The mediating role of self-efficacy and work–life balance. The International Journal of Human Resource Management, 27(15), 1755-1776.

Charmaz, K. (2006). Constructing grounded theory: A practical guide through qualitative analysis. sage.

Chen, L. (2018, April). Microservices: architecting for continuous delivery and DevOps. In 2018 IEEE International Conference on Software Architecture (ICSA) (pp. 39-397). IEEE.

Chua, C. E. H., Lim, W. K., Soh, C., & Sia, S. K. (2012). Enacting clan control in complex IT projects: A social capital perspective. MIS Quarterly, 577-600.

Chung, S., & Bang, S. (2016). Identifying knowledge, skills, and abilities (KSA) for devops-aware server-side web application with the grounded theory. Journal of Computing Sciences in Colleges, 32(1), 110-116.

Claps, G. G., Svensson, R. B., & Aurum, A. (2015). On the journey to continuous deployment: Technical and social challenges along the way. Information and Software technology, 57, 21-31.

Colomo-Palacios, R., Fernandes, E., Soto-Acosta, P., & Larrucea, X. (2018). A case analysis of enabling continuous software deployment through knowledge management. International Journal of Information Management, 40, 186-189.

Costa, P. L., Passos, A. M., & Bakker, A. B. (2014). Team work engagement: A model of emergence. Journal of Occupational and Organizational Psychology, 87(2), 414-436.

Coyle, S., Conboy, K., & Acton, T. (2013). Group process losses in agile software development decision making. International Journal of Intelligent Information Technologies (IJIIT), 9(2), 38-53.

Cram, W. A., & Newell, S. (2016). Mindful revolution or mindless trend? Examining agile development as a management fashion. European Journal of Information Systems, 25(2), 154-169.

Crotty, M. (1998). The foundations of social research: Meaning and perspective in the research process. Sage.

Creswell, J. W. (2003). Research design: Qualitative, quantitative, and mixed methods approaches. Sage publications.

Creswell, J. W. (2009). Mapping the field of mixed methods research.

Creswell, J. W. (2013). Steps in conducting a scholarly mixed methods study.

Creswell, J. W. (2014). A concise introduction to mixed methods research. SAGE publications.

Creswell, J. W., & Miller, D. L. (2000). Determining validity in qualitative inquiry. Theory into practice, 39(3), 124-130.

Cukier, D. (2013, October). DevOps patterns to scale web applications using cloud services. In Proceedings of the 2013 companion publication for conference on Systems, programming, & applications: software for humanity (pp. 143-152). ACM.

Cuppett, M. S. (2016). Devops, dbas, and dbaas: Managing data platforms to support continuous integration. Apress.

Cummings, J. N. (2004). Work groups, structural diversity, and knowledge sharing in a global organization. Management science, 50(3), 352-364.

Cunningham, H., Humphreys, K., Gaizauskas, R., & Wilks, Y. (1997, March). Software infrastructure for natural language processing. In Proceedings of the fifth conference on Applied natural language processing (pp. 237-244). Association for Computational Linguistics.

Davis, J., & Daniels, R. (2016). Effective DevOps: building a culture of collaboration, affinity, and tooling at scale. " O'Reilly Media, Inc.".

Das, B. L., & Baruah, M. (2013). Employee retention: A review of literature. Journal of Business and Management, 14(2), 8-16.

Daspit, J., Tillman, C. J., Boyd, N. G., & Mckee, V. (2013). Cross-functional team effectiveness. Team Performance Management: An International Journal.

De Bayser, M., Azevedo, L. G., & Cerqueira, R. (2015, May). ResearchOps: The case for DevOps in scientific applications. In 2015 IFIP/IEEE International Symposium on Integrated Network Management (IM) (pp. 1398-1404). IEEE.

de França, B. B. N., Jeronimo, H., & Travassos, G. H. (2016, September). Characterizing DevOps by hearing multiple voices. In Proceedings of the 30th Brazilian Symposium on Software Engineering (pp. 53-62).

Deek, F. P., & McHugh, J. A. (2007). Open source: Technology and policy. Cambridge University Press.

De Brentani, U., Kleinschmidt, E. J., & Salomo, S. (2010). Success in global new product development: Impact of strategy and the behavioral environment of the firm. Journal of product innovation management, 27(2), 143-160.

De Guinea, A. O., Webster, J., & Staples, D. S. (2012). A meta-analysis of the consequences of virtualness on team functioning. Information & Management, 49(6), 301-308.

De Jong, B. A., Dirks, K. T., & Gillespie, N. (2016). Trust and team performance: A meta-analysis of main effects, moderators, and covariates. Journal of Applied Psychology, 101(8), 1134.

Defazio, D., Lockett, A., & Wright, M. (2009). Funding incentives, collaborative dynamics and scientific productivity: Evidence from the EU framework program. Research policy, 38(2), 293-305.

Denzin, N. K., & Lincoln, Y. S. (2002). The qualitative inquiry reader. Sage.

Diel, E., Marczak, S., & Cruzes, D. S. (2016, August). Communication challenges and strategies in distributed devops. In 2016 IEEE 11th International Conference on Global Software Engineering (ICGSE) (pp. 24-28). IEEE.

Driskell, T., Salas, E., & Driskell, J. E. (2018). Teams in extreme environments: Alterations in team development and teamwork. Human Resource Management Review, 28(4), 434-449.

Driskell, J. E., Salas, E., & Driskell, T. (2018). Foundations of teamwork and collaboration. American Psychologist, 73(4), 334.

Duvall, P. (2012). Breaking down barriers and reducing cycle times with DevOps and continuous delivery. Retrieved from GigaOM Pro website: http://try. newrelic. com/rs/newrelic/images/GigaOm-Pro-Report-Breaking-down-barriersand-reducing-cycle-times-with-devops-and-continuous-delivery. pdf.

Dyck, A., Penners, R., & Lichter, H. (2015, May). Towards definitions for release engineering and DevOps. In 2015 IEEE/ACM 3rd International Workshop on Release Engineering (pp. 3-3). IEEE.

Ebert, C., Gallardo, G., Hernantes, J., & Serrano, N. (2016). DevOps. IEEE Software, 33(3), 94-100.

Endsley, M. R., & Jones, D. G. (2001, October). Disruptions, interruptions and information attack: impact on situation awareness and decision making. In Proceedings of the Human Factors and Ergonomics Society Annual Meeting (Vol. 45, No. 2, pp. 63-67). Sage CA: Los Angeles, CA: SAGE Publications.

Edwards, R., & Holland, J. (2013). What is qualitative interviewing? A&C Black.

Eisenhardt, K. M. (1989). Building theories from case study research. Academy of management review, 14(4), 532-550.

Erich, F. M. A., Amrit, C., & Daneva, M. (2017). A qualitative study of DevOps usage in practice. Journal of Software: Evolution and Process, 29(6), e1885.

Erich, F. (2018, March). DevOps is Simply Interaction Between Development and Operations. In International Workshop on Software Engineering Aspects of Continuous Development and New Paradigms of Software Production and Deployment (pp. 89-99). Springer, Cham.

Erich, F., Amrit, C., & Daneva, M. (2014). Report: Devops literature review. University of Twente, Tech. Rep.

Esterberg, K. G. (2002). Qualitative methods in social research.

Farroha, B. S., & Farroha, D. L. (2014, October). A framework for managing mission needs, compliance, and trust in the DevOps environment. In 2014 IEEE Military Communications Conference (pp. 288-293). IEEE.

Fereday, J., & Muir-Cochrane, E. (2006). Demonstrating rigor using thematic analysis: A hybrid approach of inductive and deductive coding and theme development. International journal of qualitative methods, 5(1), 80-92.

Finlay, L. (2002). Negotiating the swamp: the opportunity and challenge of reflexivity in research practice. Qualitative research, 2(2), 209-230.

Forsgren, N., & Humble, J. (2016). The role of continuous delivery in IT and organizational performance. Forsgren, N., J. Humble (2016)." The Role of Continuous Delivery in IT and Organizational Performance." In the Proceedings of the Western Decision Sciences Institute (WDSI).

Forsgren, N., & Humble, J. (2016). DevOps: Profiles in ITSM performance and contributing factors. Forsgren, N., J. Humble (2016)." DevOps: Profiles in ITSM Performance and Contributing Factors." In the Proceedings of the Western Decision Sciences Institute (WDSI).

Forsgren Velasquez, N., Kim, G., Kersten, N., & Humble, J. (2014). State of DevOps report. Puppet Labs and IT Revolution.

Forsgren, N., Tremblay, M. C., VanderMeer, D., & Humble, J. (2017, May). DORA Platform: DevOps Assessment and Benchmarking. In International Conference on Design Science Research in Information System and Technology (pp. 436-440). Springer, Cham.

Frasquet, M., Calderón, H., & Cervera, A. (2012). University–industry collaboration from a relationship marketing perspective: An empirical analysis in a Spanish University. Higher Education, 64(1), 85-98.

Ghilic-Micu, B., & Stoica, M. (2003). Trust and fear in the virtual organization. Economy Informatics, 3(24), 16-20.

Gill, A. Q., Loumish, A., Riyat, I., & Han, S. (2018). DevOps for information management systems. VINE Journal of Information and Knowledge Management Systems.

Glinow, M. A. V., & McShare, S. L. (2010). Organizational Behavior, Emerging Knowledge and Practice for Real World.

Goh, J. C. L., Pan, S. L., & Zuo, M. (2013). Developing the agile IS development practices in large-scale IT projects: The trust-mediated organizational controls and IT project team capabilities perspectives. Journal of the Association for Information Systems, 14(12), 722.

Greenberg, J., & Baron, R. A. (1995). Behavior in organizations: understanding and managing the human side of work. Englewood Cliffs, NJ: Prentice Hall.

Guchait, P. (2016). The mediating effect of team engagement between team cognitions and team outcomes in service-management teams. Journal of Hospitality & Tourism Research, 40(2), 139-161.

Gustafsson, J. (2017). Single case studies vs. multiple case studies: A comparative study.

Hackman, J. R. (1983). A normative model of work team effectiveness (No. TR-2). OFFICE OF NAVAL RESEARCH ARLINGTON VA.

Hagemann, V., & Kluge, A. (2017). Complex problem solving in teams: The impact of collective orientation on team process demands. Frontiers in psychology, 8, 1730.

Hamunen, J. (2016). Challenges in adopting a Devops approach to software development and operations.

Harter, J. K., Schmidt, F. L., & Hayes, T. L. (2002). Business-unit-level relationship between employee satisfaction, employee engagement, and business outcomes: a meta-analysis. Journal of applied psychology, 87(2), 268.

Hemon, A., Lyonnet, B., Rowe, F., & Fitzgerald, B. (2019). From Agile to DevOps: Smart Skills and Collaborations. Information Systems Frontiers, 1-19.

Hoda, R., Salleh, N., & Grundy, J. (2018). The rise and evolution of agile software development. IEEE Software, 35(5), 58-63.

Hoegl, M., & Gemuenden, H. G. (2001). Teamwork quality and the success of innovative projects: A theoretical concept and empirical evidence. Organization science, 12(4), 435-449.

Hollenbeck, J. R., Beersma, B., & Schouten, M. E. (2012). Beyond team types and taxonomies: A dimensional scaling conceptualization for team description. Academy of Management Review, 37(1), 82-106.

Hon, A. H., Bloom, M., & Crant, J. M. (2014). Overcoming resistance to change and enhancing creative performance. Journal of Management, 40(3), 919-941.

Horlach, B., Drews, P., Schirmer, I., & Böhmann, T. (2017, January). Increasing the agility of IT delivery: five types of bimodal IT organization. In Proceedings of the 50th Hawaii International Conference on System Sciences.

Howard, L. W., Turban, D. B., & Hurley, S. K. (2016). Cooperating teams and competing reward strategies: Incentives for team performance and firm productivity. Journal of Behavioral and Applied Management, 3(3), 1054.

Hu, L., & Randel, A. E. (2014). Knowledge sharing in teams: Social capital, extrinsic incentives, and team innovation. Group & Organization Management, 39(2), 213-243.

Humble, J., & Farley, D. (2010). Continuous Delivery: Reliable Software Releases through Build, Test, and Deployment Automation (Adobe Reader). Pearson Education.

Humble, J., & Molesky, J. (2011). Why enterprises must adopt devops to enable continuous delivery. Cutter IT Journal, 24(8), 6.

Humble, J. (2012). There's no such thing as a „Devops team ". Thoughtworks blog.

Hussaini, S. W. (2014, October). Strengthening harmonization of development (dev) and operations (ops) silos in it environment through systems approach. In 17th International IEEE Conference on Intelligent Transportation Systems (ITSC) (pp. 178-183). IEEE.

Hussain, W., Clear, T., & MacDonell, S. (2017, May). Emerging trends for global DevOps: a New Zealand perspective. In 2017 IEEE 12th International Conference on Global Software Engineering (ICGSE) (pp. 21-30). IEEE.

Huttermann, M. (2012). DevOps for developers. Apress.

Huysman, M., & Wulf, V. (Eds.). (2004). Social capital and information technology. Mit Press.

Ibarra, H., & Hansen, M. T. (2011). Are you a collaborative leader. Harvard business review, 89(7/8), 68-74.

Iden, J., Tessem, B., & Päivärinta, T. (2011). Problems in the interplay of development and IT operations in system development projects: A Delphi study of Norwegian IT experts. Information and Software Technology, 53(4), 394-406

Ikerionwu, C., & Edgar, D. (2016). DevOps: introducing agility and flexibility to BPO-IT organisations–service providers' perspective. Software Engineering, 4(5), 65.

Jabbari, R., bin Ali, N., Petersen, K., & Tanveer, B. (2016, May). What is devops?: A systematic mapping study on definitions and practices. In Proceedings of the Scientific Workshop Proceedings of XP2016 (p. 12). ACM.

Jia, J., Zhang, P., & Capretz, L. F. (2016, May). Environmental factors influencing individual decision-making behavior in software projects: a systematic literature review. In Proceedings of the 9th International Workshop on Cooperative and Human Aspects of Software Engineering (pp. 86-92).

Jones, M. (2019, February 25). Legal issues in DevOps. Retrieved from https://www.kemplittle.com/blog/legal-issues-in-devops/.

Jones, S., Noppen, J., & Lettice, F. (2016, July). Management challenges for DevOps adoption within UK SMEs. In Proceedings of the 2nd International Workshop on Quality-Aware DevOps (pp. 7-11). ACM.

Jordan, S. R. (2016). Positive Leadership Behavior. In A. Farazmand (Ed.), Global Encyclopedia of Public Administration, Public Policy, and Governance (pp. 1–6). https://doi.org/10.1007/978-3-319-31816-5_1341-1

Joshi, A., Lazarova, M. B., & Liao, H. (2009). Getting everyone on board: The role of inspirational leadership in geographically dispersed teams. Organization science, 20(1), 240-252.

Kahn, W. A. (2014). The student's guide to successful project teams. Routledge.

Kahn, W. A. (1990). Psychological conditions of personal engagement and disengagement at work. Academy of management journal, 33(4), 692-724

Kalliath, T., & Brough, P. (2008). Work–life balance: A review of the meaning of the balance construct. Journal of management & organization, 14(3), 323-327.

Kamuto, M. B., & Langerman, J. J. (2017, May). Factors inhibiting the adoption of DevOps in large organisations: South African context. In 2017 2nd IEEE International Conference on Recent Trends in Electronics, Information & Communication Technology (RTEICT) (pp. 48-51). IEEE.

Kim, G. (2014). The three ways: The principles underpinning DevOps.

Kim, D. H., & Lee, H. (2016). Effects of user experience on user resistance to change to the voice user interface of an in-vehicle infotainment system: Implications for platform and standards competition. International Journal of Information Management, 36(4), 653-667.

Kim, G., Behr, K., & Spafford, K. (2014). The phoenix project: A novel about IT, DevOps, and helping your business win. IT Revolution.

King, N., & Horrocks, C. (2011). Interviews in qualitative research. London: SAGE Publications Limited.

Kirsch, L. J., Ko, D. G., & Haney, M. H. (2010). Investigating the antecedents of team-based clan control: Adding social capital as a predictor. Organization Science, 21(2), 469-489.

König, L., & Steffens, A. (2018). Towards a quality model for devops. Continuous Software Engineering & Full-scale Software Engineering, 37.

Lacerenza, C. N., Marlow, S. L., Tannenbaum, S. I., & Salas, E. (2018). Team development interventions: Evidence-based approaches for improving teamwork. American Psychologist, 73(4), 517.

Lang, S. Y., Dickinson, J., & Buchal, R. O. (2002). Cognitive factors in distributed design. Computers in Industry, 48(1), 89-98.

Lee, C. J. G. (2012). Reconsidering constructivism in qualitative research. Educational Philosophy and theory, 44(4), 403-412.

Lee, S. M., Koopman, J., Hollenbeck, J. R., Wang, L. C., & Lanaj, K. (2015). The team descriptive index (TDI): A multidimensional scaling approach for team description. Academy of Management Discoveries, 1(1), 91-116.

Lick, D. W. (2006). A new perspective on organizational learning: Creating learning teams. Evaluation and Program Planning, 29(1), 88-96.

Li, Y., & Maedche, A. (2012). Formulating effective coordination strategies in agile global software development teams.

Limoncelli, T. A., & Hughe, D. (2011). LISA'11 Theme–DevOps: New Challenges, Proven Values. USENIX; login: Magazine, 36(4).

Lincoln, Y. S., Lynham, S. A., & Guba, E. G. (2011). Paradigmatic controversies, contradictions, and emerging confluences, revisited. The Sage handbook of qualitative research, 4, 97-128.

Liu, G. H., Wang, E., & Chua, C. E. H. (2015). Leveraging social capital to obtain top management support in complex, cross-functional IT projects. Journal of the Association for Information Systems, 16(8), 707.

Liu, J. Y. C., & Yuliani, A. R. (2016). Differences between clients' and vendors' perceptions of IT outsourcing risks: Project partnering as the mitigation approach. Project Management Journal, 47(1), 45-58.

Lwakatare, L. E., Kuvaja, P., & Oivo, M. (2015, May). Dimensions of devops. In International conference on agile software development (pp. 212-217). Springer, Cham.

Lwakatare, L. E., Karvonen, T., Sauvola, T., Kuvaja, P., Olsson, H. H., Bosch, J., & Oivo, M. (2016, January). Towards devops in the embedded systems domain: Why is it so hard?. In 2016 49th Hawaii International Conference on System Sciences (HICSS) (pp. 5437-5446). IEEE.

Macey, W. H., & Schneider, B. (2008). The meaning of employee engagement. Industrial and organizational Psychology, 1(1), 3-30.

Mathieu, J. E., Gilson, L. L., & Ruddy, T. M. (2006). Empowerment and team effectiveness: an empirical test of an integrated model. Journal of applied psychology, 91(1), 97.

Mack, N., Woodsong, C., MacQueen, K. M., Guest, G., & Namey, E. (2005). Qualitative research methods: a data collectors field guide.

Markey, K., Tilki, M., & Taylor, G. (2014). Reflecting on the challenges of choosing and using a grounded theory approach. Nurse researcher, 22(2).

Macnab, C. J. B., & Doctolero, S. (2019, May). The role of unconscious bias in software project failures. In International Conference on Software Engineering Research, Management and Applications (pp. 91-116). Springer, Cham.

Matook, S., & Maruping, L. M. (2014). A competency model for customer representatives in agile software development projects. MIS Quarterly Executive, 13(2).

Matturro, G., Raschetti, F., & Fontán, C. (2019). A Systematic Mapping Study on Soft Skills in Software Engineering. J. UCS, 25(1), 16-41.

Meng, A., Clausen, T., & Borg, V. (2018). The association between team-level social capital and individual-level work engagement: Differences between subtypes of social capital and the impact of intra-team agreement. Scandinavian journal of psychology, 59(2), 198-205.

Merriam, S. B. (1998). Qualitative Research and Case Study Applications in Education. Revised and Expanded from" Case Study Research in Education.". Jossey-Bass Publishers, 350 Sansome St, San Francisco, CA 94104.

Merriam, S. B. (2002). Introduction to qualitative research. Qualitative research in practice: Examples for discussion and analysis, 1(1), 1-17.

Meyer, C. B. (2001). A case in case study methodology. Field methods, 13(4), 329-352.

Myers, M. D. (2019). Qualitative research in business and management. Sage Publications Limited.

Myers, M. D., & Newman, M. (2007). The qualitative interview in IS research: Examining the craft. Information and organization, 17(1), 2-26.

Michelsen, J. (2013). Dysfunction Junction: A Pragmatic Guide to Getting Started with DevOps. CA Technologies.

Mohamed, S. I. (2015). DevOps shifting software engineering strategy-value based perspective. International Journal of Computer Engineering, 17(2), 51-57.

Mullaguru, S. N. (2015). Changing Scenario of Testing Paradigms using DevOps–A Comparative Study with Classical Models. Global Journal of Computer Science and Technology.

Nahapiet, J., & Ghoshal, S. (1998). Social capital, intellectual capital, and the organizational advantage. Academy of management review, 23(2), 242-266.

Navimipour, N. J., & Charband, Y. (2016). Knowledge sharing mechanisms and techniques in project teams: Literature review, classification, and current trends. Computers in Human Behavior, 62, 730-742.

Neuman, W. (2010). L.(2003). Social research methods: Qualitative and quantitative approaches, 5.

Neuman, W. L. (2013). Social research methods: Qualitative and quantitative approaches. Pearson education.

Nielsen, P. A., Winkler, T. J., & Nørbjerg, J. (2017). Closing the IT Development-Operations Gap: The DevOps Knowledge Sharing Framework. In BIR Workshops.

Nybom, K., Smeds, J., & Porres, I. (2016, May). On the impact of mixing responsibilities between devs and ops. In International Conference on Agile Software Development (pp. 131-143). Springer, Cham.

Onwuegbuzie, A. J., & Leech, N. L. (2007). Sampling designs in qualitative research: Making the sampling process more public. The qualitative report, 12(2), 238-254.

Palinkas, L. A., Horwitz, S. M., Green, C. A., Wisdom, J. P., Duan, N., & Hoagwood, K. (2015).

Purposeful sampling for qualitative data collection and analysis in mixed method implementation research. Administration and Policy in Mental Health and Mental Health Services Research, 42(5), 533-544.

Panteli, N., & Chiasson, M. (Eds.). (2008). Exploring virtuality within and beyond organizations: Social, global and local dimensions. Springer.

Patton, M. Q. (2002). Qualitative research and evaluation methods. Thousand Oaks. Cal.: Sage Publications.

Patton, M. Q. (2002). Two decades of developments in qualitative inquiry: A personal, experiential perspective. Qualitative social work, 1(3), 261-283.

Pardo del Val, M., & Martínez Fuentes, C. (2003). Resistance to change: a literature review and empirical study. Management decision, 41(2), 148-155.

Parker, R., & Bradley, L. (2000). Organisational culture in the public sector: evidence from six organisations. International Journal of Public Sector Management, 13(2), 125-141.

Patel, H., Pettitt, M., & Wilson, J. R. (2012). Factors of collaborative working: A framework for a collaboration model. Applied ergonomics, 43(1), 1-26.

Patwardhan, A. (2017, October). Sentiment Identification for Collaborative, Geographically Dispersed, Cross-Functional Software Development Teams. In 2017 IEEE 3rd International Conference on Collaboration and Internet Computing (CIC) (pp. 20-26). IEEE.

Paulus, P. B., & Kenworthy, J. B. (2017). Overview of team creativity and innovation. Team Creativity and Innovation, 11-38.

Pinheiro, M. L., Pinho, J. C., & Lucas, C. (2015). The outset of UI R & D relationships: the specific case of biological sciences. European Journal of Innovation Management.

Phifer, B. (2011). Next-generation process integration: CMMI and ITIL do devops. Cutter IT Journal, 24(8), 28.

Prakash, S., & Moharir, M. (2019). End to End Automation for Carrier Grade Telecom Products: A Case for DevOps.

Przybilla, L., Wiesche, M., & Krcmar, H. (2018, June). The Influence of Agile Practices on Performance in Software Engineering Teams: A Subgroup Perspective. In Proceedings of the 2018 ACM SIGMIS Conference on Computers and People Research (pp. 33-40). ACM.

Putnam, R. D. (1995). Tuning in, tuning out: The strange disappearance of social capital in America. PS: Political science & politics, 28(4), 664-683.

Rance, S. (2011). Change management. ITIL® Service Transition, 60-89.

Rajkumar, M., Pole, A. K., Adige, V. S., & Mahanta, P. (2016, April). DevOps culture and its impact on cloud delivery and software development. In 2016 International Conference on Advances in Computing, Communication, & Automation (ICACCA)(Spring) (pp. 1-6). IEEE.

Ravichandran, A., Taylor, K., & Waterhouse, P. (2016). Practical DevOps. In DevOps for Digital Leaders (pp. 125-137). Apress, Berkeley, CA.

Rawandi, A. (2009). Towards more effective management teams: Investigating the efficiency of a theoretical dynamic management model created to indicate development potentials regarding management team effectiveness.

Richards, K. (2003). Qualitative inquiry in TESOL. Springer.

Riungu-Kalliosaari, L., Mäkinen, S., Lwakatare, L. E., Tiihonen, J., & Männistö, T. (2016,

November). DevOps adoption benefits and challenges in practice: a case study. In International Conference on Product-Focused Software Process Improvement (pp. 590-597). Springer, Cham.

Riemer, K., & Klein, S. (2008). Is the V-form the next generation organisation? An Analysis of Challenges, Pitfalls and Remedies of ICT-enabled Virtual Organisations based on Social Capital Theory. Journal of Information Technology, 23(3), 147-162.

Runyan, R. C., Huddleston, P., & Swinney, J. L. (2007). A resource-based view of the small firm: Using a qualitative approach to uncover small firm resources. Qualitative Market Research: An International Journal, 10(4), 390-402.

Robert Jr, L. P., Dennis, A. R., & Ahuja, M. K. (2008). Social capital and knowledge integration in digitally enabled teams. Information systems research, 19(3), 314-334.

Rose, J., Jones, M., & Furneaux, B. (2016). An integrated model of innovation drivers for smaller software firms. Information & Management, 53(3), 307-323.

Rowlands, B. H. (2005). Grounded in practice: Using interpretive research to build theory. The Electronic Journal of Business Research Methodology, 3(1), 81-92.

Rowley, J. (2002). Using case studies in research. Management research news.

Runeson, P., Host, M., Rainer, A., & Regnell, B. (2012). Case study research in software engineering: Guidelines and examples. John Wiley & Sons.

Sacks, M. (2012). Pro Website Development and Operations: Streamlining DevOps for Large-scale Websites. Apress.

Salas, E., Cooke, N. J., & Rosen, M. A. (2008). On teams, teamwork, and team performance: Discoveries and developments. Human factors, 50(3), 540-547.

Salas, E., Dickinson, T. L., Converse, S. A., & Tannenbaum, S. I. (1992). Toward an understanding of team performance and training.

Sanchez-Gordón, M. L., Colomo-Palacios, R., & Herranz, E. (2016, September). Gamification and human factors in quality management systems: mapping from octalysis framework to ISO 10018. In European Conference on Software Process Improvement (pp. 234-241). Springer, Cham.

Sandobalin, J., Insfran, E., & Abrahao, S. (2017, June). An infrastructure modelling tool for cloud provisioning. In 2017 IEEE International Conference on Services Computing (SCC) (pp. 354-361). IEEE.

Sandoval, R. (2015). A case study in enabling DevOps using Docker (Doctoral book).

Sargeant, J. (2012). Qualitative research part II: Participants, analysis, and quality assurance.

Sarker, S., Xiao, X., & Beaulieu, T. (2013). Qualitative studies in information systems: a critical review and some guiding principles. MIS quarterly, 37(4), iii-xviii.

Saunders, M., Lewis, P., & Thornhill, A. (2009). Research methods for business students. Pearson education.

Sebastian, I. M., Ross, J. W., Beath, C., Mocker, M., Moloney, K. G., & Fonstad, N. O. (2017). How Big Old Companies Navigate Digital Transformation. MIS Quarterly Executive.

Sekaran, U., & Bougie, R. (2016). Research methods for business: A skill building approach. John Wiley & Sons.

Siggelkow, N. (2007). Persuasion with case studies. Academy of management journal, 50(1), 20-24.

Senapathi, M., Buchan, J., & Osman, H. (2018, June). DevOps capabilities, practices, and challenges: Insights from a case study. In Proceedings of the 22nd International Conference on Evaluation and Assessment in Software Engineering 2018 (pp. 57-67). ACM.

Shahin, M. (2015, September). Architecting for devops and continuous deployment. In Proceedings of the ASWEC 2015 24th Australasian Software Engineering Conference (pp. 147-148). ACM.

Shahin, M., Babar, M. A., & Zhu, L. (2017). Continuous integration, delivery and deployment: a systematic review on approaches, tools, challenges and practices. IEEE Access, 5, 3909-3943.

Shahin, M., Zahedi, M., Babar, M. A., & Zhu, L. (2017, June). Adopting continuous delivery and deployment: Impacts on team structures, collaboration and responsibilities. In Proceedings of the 21st International Conference on Evaluation and Assessment in Software Engineering (pp. 384-393). ACM.

Sharma, S. (2017). The DevOps Adoption Playbook: A Guide to Adopting DevOps in a Multi-Speed IT Enterprise. John Wiley & Sons.

Shenton, A. K. (2004). Strategies for ensuring trustworthiness in qualitative research projects. Education for information, 22(2), 63-75.

Shropshire, J., & Sweeney, B. (2017). On Devops and Workforce Morale. SAIS 2017 Proceedings.

Simon, H. A. and March, J. G. (1967) Organisations, Graduate School of Industrial Administration, Carnegie Institute of Technology.

Small, M. (2017). Analysis of an organisation: A University of the third age (U3A), Mornington, Victoria. Australian Journal of Adult Learning, 57(1), 147.

Smeds, J., Nybom, K., & Porres, I. (2015, May). DevOps: a definition and perceived adoption impediments. In International Conference on Agile Software Development (pp. 166-177). Springer, Cham.

Smith, P. A., Bakker, M., Leenders, R. T. A., Gabbay, S. M., Kratzer, J., & Van Engelen, J. M. (2006). Is trust really social capital? Knowledge sharing in product development projects. The Learning Organization.

Smith, M. B., Wallace, J. C., Vandenberg, R. J., & Mondore, S. (2018). Employee involvement climate, task and citizenship performance, and instability as a moderator. The International Journal of Human Resource Management, 29(4), 615-636.

Smith-Jentsch, K. A., Mathieu, J. E., & Kraiger, K. (2005). Investigating linear and interactive effects of shared mental models on safety and efficiency in a field setting. Journal of applied psychology, 90(3), 523.

Smite, D., Moe, N. B., Šāblis, A., & Wohlin, C. (2017). Software teams and their knowledge networks in large-scale software development. Information and Software Technology, 86, 71-86.

Solutions, C., & Infrastructure, I. T. Build a DevOps culture and team Building a culture is at the core of adopting the IBM Garage Method for Cloud.

Sozbilir, F. (2018). The interaction between social capital, creativity and efficiency in organizations. Thinking Skills and Creativity, 27, 92-100.

Stahl, D., Mårtensson, T., & Bosch, J. (2017). The continuity of continuous integration: correlations and consequences. Journal of Systems and Software, 127, 150-167.

Stahl, D., Martensson, T., & Bosch, J. (2017, August). Continuous practices and devops:

beyond the buzz, what does it all mean? In 2017 43rd Euromicro Conference on Software Engineering and Advanced Applications (SEAA) (pp. 440-448). IEEE.

Stock, R. (2004). Drivers of team performance: What do we know and what have we still to learn? Schmalenbach Business Review, 56(3), 274-306.

Stray, V., Moe, N. B., & Aasheim, A. (2019, January). Dependency management in large-scale agile: a case study of DevOps teams. In Proceedings of the 52nd Hawaii International Conference on System Sciences.

Stray, V., Moe, N. B., & Hoda, R. (2018, May). Autonomous agile teams: Challenges and future directions for research. In Proceedings of the 19th International Conference on Agile Software Development: Companion (p. 16). ACM.

Strode, D. E. (2016). A dependency taxonomy for agile software development projects. Information Systems Frontiers, 18(1), 23-46.

Srivastava, A., Bartol, K. M., & Locke, E. A. (2006). Empowering leadership in management teams: Effects on knowledge sharing, efficacy, and performance. Academy of management journal, 49(6), 1239-1251.

Sun, S. (2008). Organizational culture and its themes. International Journal of Business and Management, 3(12), 137-141.

Stake, R. E. (1995). The art of case study research. Thousand Oaks, CA: Sage.

Stock, R. (2004). Drivers of team performance: What do we know and what have we still to learn? Schmalenbach Business Review, 56(3), 274-306.

Swartout, P. (2018). Continuous Delivery and DevOps–A Quickstart Guide: Start your journey to successful adoption of CD and DevOps. Packt Publishing Ltd.

Tanner, M., & von Willingh, U. (2014). Factors leading to the success and failure of agile projects implemented in traditionally waterfall environments. Human Capital without Borders: Knowledge and Learning for the Quality of Life. Portoroz, Slovenia: Make Learn.

Tessem, B., & Iden, J. (2008, May). Cooperation between developers and operations in software engineering projects. In Proceedings of the 2008 international workshop on Cooperative and human aspects of software engineering (pp. 105-108). ACM.

Todino, A., Viglietti, I., Tranchero, B., & de Juan-Marín, R. (2016). Designing a System Engineering Environment in a Structured Way. In CIISE (pp. 31-39).

Tsai, W., & Ghoshal, S. (1998). Social capital and value creation: The role of intrafirm networks. Academy of management Journal, 41(4), 464-476.

Tsoukas, H., & Knudsen, C. (2003). Introduction: The need for meta-theoretical reflection in organization theory. In The Oxford handbook of organization theory (pp. 1-36). Oxford University Press.

Tymon, W. G., & Stumpf, S. A. (2003). Social capital in the success of knowledge workers. Career Development International, 8(1), 12-20.

Van den Broeck, A., Sulea, C., Vander Elst, T., Fischmann, G., Iliescu, D., & De Witte, H. (2014). The mediating role of psychological needs in the relation between qualitative job insecurity and counterproductive work behavior. Career Development International.

van Ommeren, E., van Doorn, M., Dial, J., & van Herpes, D. (2018). Mastering Digital Disruption with DevOps.

Von Treuer, K. (2013). Group and team processes in organisations. Organisational psychology research and professional practice, 269-295.

Volti, R. (2009). Society and technological change. New York: Worth Publishers.

Wagner, H. T., Beimborn, D., & Weitzel, T. (2014). How social capital among information technology and business units drives operational alignment and IT business value. Journal of Management Information Systems, 31(1), 241-272.

Waller, J., Ehmke, N. C., & Hasselbring, W. (2015). Including performance benchmarks into continuous integration to enable DevOps. ACM SIGSOFT Software Engineering Notes, 40(2), 1-4.

Walls, M. (2013). Building a DevOps culture. " O'Reilly Media, Inc.".

Wang, C., & Liu, C. (2018). Adopting DevOps in Agile: Challenges and Solutions.

Wegner, D. M. (1995). A computer network model of human transactive memory. Social cognition, 13(3), 319-339.

Wettinger, J., Andrikopoulos, V., & Leymann, F. (2015, March). Automated capturing and systematic usage of devops knowledge for cloud applications. In 2015 IEEE International Conference on Cloud Engineering (pp. 60-65). IEEE.

White, H. C. (2019). Careers and creativity: Social forces in the arts. Routledge.

Wiedemann, A. M., & Schulz, T. (2017). Key Capabilities of DevOps teams and their influence on software process innovation: a resource-based view.

Wiedemann, A. (2018, January). IT Governance Mechanisms for DevOps Teams-How Incumbent Companies Achieve Competitive Advantages. In Proceedings of the 51st Hawaii International Conference on System Sciences.

Wiedemann, A., & Weeger, A. (2017). Developing Intellectual Capital within Agile IT Teams: A Literature Review.

Wiedemann, A., Wiesche, M., & Krcmar, H. (2019, June). Integrating Development and Operations in Cross-Functional Teams-Toward a DevOps Competency Model. In Proceedings of the 2019 on Computers and People Research Conference (pp. 14-19). ACM.

Wiedemann, A., Forsgren, N., Wiesche, M., Gewald, H., & Krcmar, H. (2019). The DevOps Phenomenon. Queue, 17(2), 40.

Wiedemann, A., Gewald, H., Krcmar, H., & Wiesche, M. (2019). The DevOps Phenomenon: An Executive Crash Course.

Wiedemann, A., Wiesche, M., Gewald, H., & Kremar, H. (2018). Integrating DevOps within IT Organizations-Key Pattern of a Case Study.

Wildman, J. L., Shuffler, M. L., Lazzara, E. H., Fiore, S. M., Burke, C. S., Salas, E., & Garven, S. (2012). Trust development in swift starting action teams: A multilevel framework. Group & Organization Management, 37(2), 137-170.

Wiesche, M., & Krcmar, H. (2014, May). The relationship of personality models and development tasks in software engineering. In Proceedings of the 52nd ACM conference on Computers and people research (pp. 149-161). ACM.

Wiedemann, A., & Wiesche, M. (2018). Are you ready for Devops? Required skill set for Devops teams. In Proceedings of the European Conference on Information Systems.

Wurster, L. F., Colville, R. J., Haight, C., Tripathi, S., & Rastogi, A. (2013). Emerging technology analysis: DevOps a culture shift not a technology. Gartner.

Yiran, Z., & Yilei, L. (2017). The Challenges and Mitigation Strategies of Using DevOps during Software Development.

Yin, R. K. (2003). Case study research: Design and methods. Thousand Oaks, CA: Sage

Publications. Politics of Education Association Bulletin.

Yin, R. K. (2009). Case study research: Design and methods (applied social research methods). London and Singapore: Sage.

Young, R., & Jordan, E. (2008). Top management support: Mantra or necessity. International journal of project management, 26(7), 713-725.

Zambonelli, F., Jennings, N. R., & Wooldridge, M. (2000, June). Organisational abstractions for the analysis and design of multi-agent systems. In International Workshop on Agent-Oriented Software Engineering (pp. 235-251). Springer, Berlin, Heidelberg.

Zhang, Y. (2016). Functional diversity and group creativity: The role of group longevity. The Journal of Applied Behavioral Science, 52(1), 97-123.

Zheng, Y. (2012). Unlocking founding team prior shared experience: A transactive memory system perspective. Journal of Business Venturing, 27(5), 577-591.

Zoltan, R. (2012). A conceptual framework for team social capital as basis for organizational team synergy. Economics and Applied Informatics. 2, I, Annals of Dunarea de jos University of Galati, 123-132.

Zweni, T. (2004). An assessment of the impact of organisational restructuring on the morale of employees at a selected financial institution (Doctoral book, Nelson Mandela Metropolitan University).

Appendices

Appendix A: Request for Permission

Date: 20 September 2018

The Chief Information Officer
Telcom Organisation
Telkom Data Centre
23 Teddington Rd
Bellville
Cape Town

Dear Mr. September

RE: REQUEST FOR PERMISSION TO CONDUCT RESEARCH

I am a registered Masters student in the Department of Information Systems, Faculty of Commerce at the University of Cape Town. My supervisor is Maureen Tanner (contact details provided upon request).

My research topic is: **Factors that influence the synergy between Development and IT Operations in a DevOps Environment.**

The primary objective is to identify the factors that influence the synergy between development and IT operations within a DevOps environment. The primary objective will be fulfilled through the achievement of the following the following:

- Identifying which factors promote the synergy between development and IT operations.

- Identifying which factors inhibit the synergy between development and IT operations.

I am hereby seeking your consent to perform my research at your organisation. To assist you in reaching a decision, I have attached to this letter: a copy of an ethical clearance certificate issued by the University and copy the research instruments which I intend using in my research.

Should you require any further information, please do not hesitate to contact me or my supervisor. Upon completion of the study, I undertake to provide you with a copy of the final research report.

Your favourable response towards this request will be greatly appreciated.

Yours sincerely,
Arther Dinner
Student

Appendix B: Interview Questions

The interviews questions will be classified into nine categories i.e. a general section, which responds to questions about the participant's role, and the other sections are derived from constructs of the chosen theoretical framework addressing the main research question and the sub-questions discussed in section 4 as follows:

- **Main RQ**: What are the factors that influence the synergy between software development and IT operations in a DevOps environment?

- **Sub Question 1**: What factors are enablers of relational, structural and cognitive dimensions of social capital as a basis for team synergy between development and IT operations?

- **Sub Question 2**: What factors are inhibitors of relational, structural and cognitive dimensions of social capital as a basis for team synergy between development and IT operations?

A. General Information

- What is your job title or role?

- What is your responsibility?

- What is your experience working on DevOps projects?

- How is the work in your DevOps team organized?

B. Environmental

- What constraints have you encountered in your working environment?

- How do these constraints affect the dimensions of team social capital?

- What kind of extreme environment conditions exist in your working area?

- How does the current environment promote or prevent team synergy?

C. Organisational

- What is the role of your organisation in promoting or preventing team synergy?

- How often does the organization structure change and how does it affect the dimensions of team social capital?

- What effect does the organization's functional boundaries (roles and responsibilities) have on the dimensions of team social capital?

D. Team Characteristics

- Are all your DevOps team members located in the room?

- How does that impact on the dimensions of team social capital?

E. Characteristics of Individual Team Members

- Describe the importance of your skills in your working domain and to other team members?

- How flexible are you working with new team members?

- What are your key competencies?

- How do you contribute to the dimensions of team social capital?

F. Task Characteristics

- Describe the nature and structure of your work?

- How does the nature and structure of your work contribute towards the dimensions of team social capital?

- How do you deal with task dependencies within your team?

G. Team Processes

- What processes are in place to support the team synergy between development and operations?

- Discuss how the following processes are carried out in your team:

    o   Leadership behavior

    o   Communication

    o   Conflict resolution

    o   Decision-making

- How does the use of these team processes prevent or promote the dimensions of team social capital?

H. Use of Technology

- What technologies are used in your team to collaborate work activities?

- What effect does these technologies have on the dimensions of team social capital?

I. Knowledge Sharing

- How is knowledge shared between the development and operations teams?

- What kind of information is shared and how does is it affect the synergy and interactions between the development and operations?

- What platforms are used by development and operations in support of knowledge sharing?

- What is the contribution of knowledge sharing towards the dimensions of team social capital?

Appendix C: Observation Report Structure

Observation Number: ....
Date and Time: ....

Activities Observed: ....
....
....
....
....
....
....
....

Researcher's Notes/Comments: ....
....
....
....
....
....
....

Appendix D: Consent to Participate

To: XXX-Interview Participant
From: Arther Dinner
Subject: Consent to Participate
Date: 20 September 2018

Dear: XXX-P

My name is Arther Dinner, and I am a Masters student at the University of Cape Town. I am investigating the factors that influence the synergy between Development and IT operations in a DevOps environment. I am mainly interested in addressing these research questions: (1) What are the factors that influence the synergy between Development and IT Operations in a DevOps environment; (2) What factors are enablers or inhibitors of relational, structural and cognitive dimensions of social capital as the basis for team synergy.

This research will contribute to the body of knowledge on DevOps teams about how they can achieve team effectiveness and performance through synergy. The research could probably assist with a greater appreciation of the success of DevOps teams and could raise the interest of organizations in the adoption of DevOps practices in the future.

Your participation is voluntary. You do not have to respond to any questions you do not feel like responding. If at any point you are not willing to proceed with the interview, you may decline. Your participation is deeply welcomed. The interview session will take approximately 45 minutes to an hour. To maintain the core of your words for the study, I will record the information. At any time, you may ask to see or listen to the recorded information. I will give you a call within 2 days to schedule a suitable time for the interview at your premises.

The interview will be recorded, and the interviewer will make notes for data analysis. The audio record will be transcribed by the interviewer and stored in a password-protected file for confidentiality. Citations from the interview may be included in the final report or other future deliverables. However, your real name will not appear in these deliverables.

I would be appreciative if you would confirm by signing the form on the line provided below to indicate that you have read and agree with the contents. Please reply to me by email at DNNART001@myuct.ac.za.

____

Sign above

This research is being conducted to fulfil requirements for my Masters of Commerce (Information Systems) degree at the University of Cape Town.
Sincerely,

Arther Dinner
UCT Student

www.ingramcontent.com/pod-product-compliance
Lightning Source LLC
LaVergne TN
LVHW041709190726
843493LV00007B/2017